shepherds of coyote rocks

A ewe cleans her newborn lamb as it enjoys the spring sunshine.

shepherds of coyote rocks

CAT URBIGKIT

The Countryman Press
Woodstock, Vermont

*In honor of the animals and people
inhabiting working landscapes
around the world.*

All photographs: © Cat Urbigkit

Book design and composition by S. E. Livingston

Published by The Countryman Press, P.O. Box 748, Woodstock, VT 05091

Distributed by W. W. Norton & Company, Inc., 500 Fifth Avenue, New York, NY 10110

Printed in the United States of America

10 9 8 7 6 5 4 3 2 1

contents

prologue

◇ ◇ ◇ ◇

The wind is picking up—as I write, the candle flickers, the herding dog at my feet erupts into nervous shivers, and I can feel the camper's gentle rocking as wind gusts pelt its sides. Despite the swaying, I feel as though I'm in a safe cocoon, tucked as we are into the side of a hill facing the magnificent jagged peaks of the Wind River Mountains.

I came to this range with my sheep because it was the natural thing to do, although that might seem like an odd thought for an American woman. I started my sheep herd fifteen years ago. Escaping the close confines of town life, we'd leased an old ranch and wanted to retain its agricultural tax status. When a sheep rancher offered me the opportunity to try my hand with sheep by raising orphan lambs, I'd soon swooned over those beautiful babes.

Those lambs grew up and my family followed them as they grazed, noticing which plants they favored and wondering why. My husband, Jim, even tasted the plants they gravitated to during various seasons. His study of the vegetation and its nutritional content gave him an understanding, a new sort of knowledge. In our close observation of the sheep, we found ourselves in a more intimate relationship with the land, with nature, and the life supported by our range. I watched the pronghorn antelope migrate through our pasture early in the spring as they moved north, and watched again as the herds passed by in their fall movement to the south. It's a natural seasonal shift made by all the wild ungulates in this region, with migrations based on the seasons and food sources. In contrast, my sheep stayed in one place.

When the opportunity arose, through an arrangement with an-

Overleaf: A ewe and her lamb stand atop Coyote Rocks.

I began my herd by raising orphan lambs.

other sheep producer, for my now much larger sheep herd to move to open rangeland, following at least a portion of nature's pattern of migration with the seasons, I jumped at the chance. I would stay with the herd for lambing and grazing through the spring and summer seasons, sharing the experience the way my Nepalese friends do with their larger herds nearby. My Basque friend Pete owns a large sheep outfit and employs herders from a small village in Nepal to guide his sheep from lowland deserts in the winter to high in the Wind River Mountains in the summer. I'd known these herders for years, working alongside them on occasion as we helped out on Pete's ranch, learning much about sheep in the process.

Our season on the range would be more than an adventure. It would determine whether my family would be able to continue in the ranching business. I had given up a job in town to make this venture into living with livestock, something Jim and I had yearned for, for dozens of years. We were both raised in agriculture, but my family had lost our farm in the farm crisis that crept across America like a toxic plague in the 1970s, wiping out the hopes and dreams of rural families across the nation. Jim's future on his family's farm befell the same fate as those of many others: as older generations pass on, inheritance taxes and divisions of property eat up farm acreage until the farms are no longer viable units for the heirs who were raised on that ancestral soil.

I had come to develop a deep connection to the gentle, trusting creatures that made up our herd. I had bottle-fed orphan lambs as they lay shivering across my lap, looking intently into my eyes as though they were peering deep inside my soul. There were those I couldn't save, that died in my arms, a slight sigh the only indication that life had left their frail bodies. Those that survived grew from skinny, long-legged babes into large ewes weighing nearly two hundred pounds, the very definition of maternal in their roundness, some calling out to me in greeting as we met each new day.

Raising sheep had become more than my livelihood—it had become my life, an essential part of my identity. In my close association with the herd, I would learn my own lessons about life, observing the bond formed between a newborn lamb and its mother; the panic that ensues when a ewe goes astray and can't find her flock; the pure joy exhibited by a gang of energetic lambs; and the comfort of having companions you can rely on always nearby. In accompanying the herd here, I had gone from simply raising sheep to being a shepherd, one whose own welfare was intimately connected to the welfare of the flock. One who would give anything to protect it.

The decision to move the herd to open rangeland along the Rocky Mountain front wasn't taken lightly; I knew the responsibility was immense. There would be no safety like that offered by small paddocks and warm barns. The tradeoff would be in freedom. The sheep would have the opportunity to be the animals they are meant to be, to move, to graze, to water, to roam about the landscape as they pleased, with

Small lambs begin to dot the landscape.

On the open range, my sheep will trade the safety of paddocks and warm barns for freedom.

me as their companion, their shepherd. They would live much as wild creatures, and much like their ovine relatives around the world, both wild and domestic. They would grow fatter each day, foraging on the highly nutritious vegetation growing in this high-elevation desert.

It would be my job to assist lambs stuck in bogs, to tend to the wounds of the injured, to keep the sheep away from poisonous weeds or stagnant water, to help the herd escape biting flies and gnats, to nurture the sick, young, or weak, and to protect them from harm. I would guide the herd to good grazing, to clean water, and to beds in quiet places for restful sleep, free from fear. My first thoughts in the morning would be the safekeeping of the sheep, as would be my last thoughts at night. I would awaken to the sounds of the night, listening for any indication of distress. Even in my sleep, I would tend to the sheep. I was thankful I would be sharing the job of watching over the herd with our livestock protection dogs. The dogs could mean the difference between success and failure.

Jim, meanwhile, would keep the home fire burning, between his job in town and running supplies to my camp. I would see him one evening a week, and he would join me in camp for the weekends. Our son Cass was completing his first year of college, and would soon arrive back in the area to work at a nearby ranch for summer break, determined to prove himself to the outside world. I would rejoin Jim at home in the fall, when we would ship the year's lamb crop to market, the ewe flock returned to our home ranch. I hoped it would be a time to celebrate the success of the season.

Success on the range meant survival. Ewes would give birth to viable lambs that would thrive and grow, with most of the lambs sold in the fall, providing enough support for another year in this beautiful landscape, with just a little extra to allow the herd to grow. Failure would mean that we'd succumbed to the natural threats that awaited us, with loss of life to ewes and lambs. Disaster could come in a variety of forms—from blizzards to lightning strikes to large predators. If disaster befell the herd, it befell me as well. If I failed, the sheep would be sold and we would begin a new chapter in life—one without the herd. I was excited about the adventure ahead, but well aware of the seriousness of the undertaking.

CHAPTER 1

to the range

◇ ◇ ◇ ◇

The land outside my door is a land of contrasts. Today it is a place of supple beauty, the quiet of dawn punctuated only by the soft call of a golden eagle on her rock perch half a mile away, and the *quork, quork* of a murder of ravens as they fly over, inspecting my outpost. Yet while the sunlight spreads its golden rays over my nestled camp, I look up to see a winter storm raging over the granite peaks in the distance, the highline buried in a startling ribbon of white. I'm only an hour from our home ranch, but it's as though I'm on the other side of the world. The landscape resembles the steppes of Mongolia. In fact, today it feels like Mongolia. I know this, having been drawn to the Mongolian steppe, and feeling at home in that amber Asian light.

Like the Mongolian nomads whose lives are tied to the herds they tend, I am here to watch over my sheep. I am alone in camp, with one herding dog, three guardian dogs, and several hundred pregnant ewes. The sheep are slated to begin giving birth in less than a week, and it's my responsibility to shepherd them, to keep them safe. There are no houses within view, no lights at night to mar the pristine darkness other than that of the moon, the stars, and my flickering candle.

We're new to the neighborhood, having trucked the sheep in yesterday, the first of May. We've received many shy visitors in the hours since our arrival, most in the form of curious avians, fluttering, flickering, hovering above, checking out the newcomers. Yesterday, despite the gusting winds of late afternoon, we were greeted by the smallest of the falcons, an American kestrel. A fluttering of wings above the bedded sheep, the kestrel zigzagged just out of reach. Small groups of

Overleaf: Pregnant ewes graze a hillside under dusk's amber light.

Guardian love

pronghorn antelope raced in to see the new ungulates on their range, only to come to an abrupt halt, snorting their displeasure at our trespass. The pronghorn gradually calmed, pointing their dramatically marked faces to the ground, nibbling the fresh spring growth, succumbing to an acceptance of shared range.

I take comfort in the fact that, forty miles to the south, sheepherders from Nepal tend to other herds grazing this sagebrush range. They are my comrades, kindred spirits. They may have left extended families—their wives, small children, aunts, uncles, cousins, parents, and grandparents—back home in Nepal; they may have once been mercenaries fighting for whoever could pay the most; they may currently be small-businesspeople working in a global climate. No matter their background, this nomadic shepherd life drew them here.

We each have our own stories. This is mine, a season with the sheep.

The wind howled through part of our first night on the range, but when it calmed, I looked out from my warm sleeping bag to discover a bright waning moon lighting up the landscape. Coyotes were howling and yowling in the badlands and clay buttes to the southeast, and my livestock guardian dogs were returning the barrage of sound. I would find sleep difficult in silence, but the low, full-throated boom of a large dog is akin to rocking my cradle.

At dawn I rose to check the sheep, which were contentedly moving off their bedding ground, tasting the morning's frosty morsels, and the livestock guardian dogs began to appear around camp. First Rena, the ambassador of all guardians, came in with enthusiasm, apparently pleased to learn that I had endured the night. Next came the young stud dog, our Russian comrade Rant, limping up from the hills below, stiff and sore, a battle-weary warrior. Luv's Girl, the oldest and wisest, mother of Rena, trotted in hungry, arising from her bed amid the sheep. Each received fresh water and food along with my adoration. The dogs are tired this morning, and I can only hope that the coyotes are feeling the same way.

Jim called my cell phone (I have cell service only atop the highest hills of this remote rangeland), reporting that the weather would be blustery for the next two days, with a good probability of rain or snow on the third day. Since the morning was fairly calm, I decided after

Coyotes are a constant presence on the rangeland,
keeping our guardians on alert.

breakfast to take the sheep to the only water hole in the pasture, before the winds began again. The herd had been quenching its thirst
on snowdrifts remaining in a few gullies and draws, and with the
morning frost on their grazing range. Rena and Abe, my herding dog
and constant companion, came along, helping me move the herd to
water. The sheep are naturally wary about walking into tall brush and
always pause on hills to scope out the scene below before proceed-
ing. Rena took the lead, scouting out ahead of the herd as Abe and I

directed from behind. In her position up front, Rena flushed a few sage grouse and chased off the ravens that swooped low overhead.

We arrived at the small impoundment only to find a layer of ice on the surface. While Rena and I got busy busting ice along the edge, the herd proceeded forward, not the slightest bit interested in our efforts. Apparently the morning frost provided all the moisture the animals needed, but at least they would know where to find water later on.

We hurried to catch up, as the sheep grazed atop a mound I had dubbed Coyote Rocks, where golden eagles, sly coyotes, and elusive desert cottontails live a secretive existence. Abe, Rena, and I spent the next hour climbing around, inspecting all the nooks, caves, nests, and dens. The multicolored lichen blanketing the rocks is abundant, as are the whitewash stains left by raptors on their most-frequented perches. The wind resumed its howling while we were thus engaged, with the sheep grazing away from us down below. We made it back to camp just as the clouds moved over us, casting the landscape in shadow, accompanied by gusting cold winds.

The rangeland we inhabit is in the Big Sandy region of western Wyoming, part of the Upper Green River basin. The basin encompasses hundreds of square miles of land, ranging from the high-elevation granite Wind River Mountains, to boulder-strewn foothills, sagebrush steppe, and semiarid desert. The Green River emerges from the Wind River Mountains and flows south through the basin to Wyoming's border with Utah and Colorado. Farther south, the river merges with the Colorado River, which traverses the western states to its end in Mexico.

Although there are small towns and ranches in this basin, wildlife and livestock vastly outnumber people. It is a part of the West sometimes called the Empty Interior—thousands of miles of arid and semiarid landscapes that were never fully settled for permanent residency, but traditionally used by drovers for seasonal livestock grazing. Deemed undesirable for settlement, these areas were declared public lands, to be managed by federal authorities, with grazing as their primary use.

Grazing privileges are parceled out under a federal permitting sys-

Rena patrols the pasture under threatening skies.

tem, with set durations and conditions for use. A federal grazing allotment can be a series of pastures ranging in size from a few acres to dozens of square miles. Some allotments are species-specific (intended only for sheep or cattle, for example), while others can be grazed by various herds. Some allotments provide for grazing by one ranch, while others, called common allotments, allow numerous ranches (often in the form of grazing associations) to combine their livestock and graze their animals together.

The rangeland my sheep are inhabiting this year encompasses nearly thirty square miles. The smallest pasture is only a few square miles, and fenced on all sides. The other pastures are up to seventeen square miles in expanse, with fences on two sides, a wide western river as one boundary, and a wet draw as its remaining border. Along with shepherding the flock through the grazing season, seeing that my sheep partake of the natural bounty and the water sources available as conditions change, I am also tasked with keeping the herd within its defined range.

The seasonal movement of livestock with their human tenders is called transhumance, and it is practiced throughout the world. I am one of a global population of fifty million shepherds. My kin may be bronzed Kazakhs, or black-skinned Africans, dark-haired Spaniards, brown-eyed Indians, or olive-skinned Basques, but it's no matter—our similarities are greater than our differences. They are my people.

In southwestern Afghanistan, the Kuchi nomads move from semi-desert areas in the winter into highland regions for summer grazing of their sheep and goat herds, which they raise for meat, wool, milk, and cheese. They also raise donkeys and camels for transportation, so one family may tend to four types of stock. At least one-third of all sheep and goats in Afghanistan are raised in a transhumance system, a natural process of livestock production. These nomad pastoralists keep their animals on the move, which protects local resources from overgrazing.

The Kuchi also raise livestock guardian dogs, large mastiff- or Ovcharka-type beasts that move with the herds and are treasured for their ability to kill wolves, which threaten both livestock and people. The British diplomat and adventurer Rory Stewart had one of these dogs accompany him on his walk across Afghanistan, as recounted in his fascinating 2004 book, *The Places In Between*.

A local man who escorted Stewart through a mountainous region of Afghanistan carried a gun on the journey. When Stewart asked why, the man explained: "Six months ago on that slope on my way to vaccinate some of the sheep on that hill, I came across the clothes and then the leg of a friend who had just been eaten by a wolf in the middle of the day. Two years ago, five wolves killed my neighbor at eleven in the morning."

Our continued legal morass of wolf management in the United States is so incredibly far removed from other people, other cultures, who live with wolves in an intimate way. Dueling interests in America have battled their disputes out in the court systems for decades, arguing whether wolves should be managed by state or federal officials, or hunted or not, with one plan and decision seemingly leading only to another lawsuit. Little of the debate has anything to do with the reality of living with wolves on the landscape.

In the twentieth century there was an exodus of humans from

Both wild and domestic herds use the same ancient trailing routes in seasonal movements.

Europe's Pyrenees Mountains, and large parts of the lowlands were set aside for conservation purposes, with reintroductions and expansions of populations of a wide variety of wildlife species, including large carnivores such as bears and wolves. Much of the agricultural use of the mountain region declined, and agriculturalists remaining in the area were faced with wildlife populations that adversely impacted their livelihoods but remained fully protected. Outsiders who value conservation and ecotourism over local subsistence are in ef-

fect dictating management regimes to the detriment of the humans who live there. It doesn't seem like a good path to follow.

Coyotes are our most frequent predator, providing challenges to our livestock protection dogs on a daily basis. Although they are often seen hunting alone for small animals such as voles, mice, pocket gophers, and grouse, they also hunt in packs, especially in winter when pack size can include six or seven animals as they try for larger game.

In a study conducted at Yellowstone National Park, wildlife researchers found coyotes were successful in taking down adult elk and mule deer in five of nine attempts. The prey animals escaped into water in three of the four unsuccessful hunts. But Yellowstone, some two hundred miles north of the rangeland my herd and I inhabit, is an exceptional place, where the largest coyote pack ever recorded roamed one recent winter, consisting of ten adults and twelve pups. Free from human persecution or harvest, wildlife populations have thrived in the park, allowing some populations to expand in size or densities unseen elsewhere.

Mark Twain penned a telling description of the coyote in his western travel tale *Roughing It,* calling it "a long, slim, sick and sorry looking skeleton, with a gray wolf skin stretched over it, a tolerably bushy tail that forever sags down with a despairing expression of forsakenness and misery, a furtive and evil eye, and a long sharp face, with a slightly lifted lip and exposed teeth. He has a general slinking appearance all over. The cayote [*sic*] is a living, breathing allegory of Want. He is always poor, out of luck, and friendless. The meanest creatures despise him, and even the fleas would desert him for a velocipede. He is so spiritless and cowardly that even while his exposed teeth are pretending a threat, the rest of his face is apologizing for it. And he is so homely, so scrawny, and ribby, and coarse-haired, and pitiful."

One spring day at the home ranch, my son Cass and I watched a coyote go after a newborn pronghorn fawn in our hay meadow next to the New Fork River. Its mother reacted with a vengeance, striking out at the coyote with her front hooves. From our truck we watched as the doe continued running at the coyote and lunging at him until he escaped into the river to evade her wrath.

Although they can appear large, most adult coyotes in this basin weigh only twenty to thirty-five pounds, with a thick pelage hiding their light bone structure. Even so, coyotes are the principal predator on domestic sheep flocks in the West, accounting for 70 percent of total predator losses. When a sheepman refers to a person as a coyote, it's the ultimate insult.

Coyotes breed early in the year (January to March), whelping an average of six pups sixty days later. Pups are fed on milk for about three weeks, and then they begin to eat regurgitated food provided by both parents. This is also about the time they begin emerging from the den, which coincides with domestic sheep beginning to give birth to their lambs out on the range.

Pups will begin dispersal at about five months of age, but their home ranges usually remain within their mother's home range, ex panding out as the pups age. According to Canadian researchers, a single home range may be inhabited by a family of two or more generations. The small predators are known to live up to about fifteen years. When I contemplate the knowledge inherent in that coyote family group, inhabiting the same range, generation after generation, I'm awed.

Coyotes are smart, efficient predators. Many stories have been told of them teaming up in groups to hunt together, and there are numerous accounts of coyotes joining in cooperative hunting ventures with badgers. Cunning animals, but social when it's beneficial.

Throughout the year, we use a variety of methods and techniques to keep the damage from coyotes and other predators to a minimum. Our sheep flock closely together and move as one, which is a predator defense mechanism. (Lone sheep off by themselves become coyote food.) Our rams, which are placed with the ewes in December and remain there through the winter, have horns and know how to use them. Our ewes are big and will defend their young, striking out with their front hooves at a threat. We use both livestock protection dogs and burros. My frequent presence with the herd is also a deterrent. I shoot a lot, making noise to keep predators at bay. We are careful not to leave sick, injured, or dead sheep on the range, and the dogs will clean up the sheep's afterbirth during lambing, reducing potential predator attractants. We do even more at the home ranch, but we still wind up with problems. Typically it's with coyotes, but we also have problems with wolves and bears. Yes, even out in the sagebrush rangelands we encounter these predators. Not most people's idea of large-carnivore habitat, but river bottoms make for prime wildlife-migration corridors.

I stayed awake late last night reading, and just minutes after I shut off the light, the coyotes began yowling, calling the dogs out to the hills below my camp. Since coyotes typically try to enter the herd under cover of darkness, this is when our dogs do battle with them; few physical conflicts are seen by human eyes. I listened to hear the outcome of the dispute, but the wind didn't allow much satisfaction to that end. Within another hour, the wind increased in earnest, such that I curled into my warm bed and hoped that the gusts that were rocking the camp wouldn't blow us to Kansas or some other distant place. I later learned that a wind gust of more than 110 miles an hour was recorded on a ridge across the basin. The wind certainly wasn't that bad in my camp, owing to its placement tucked into the hillside.

When I arose to check the sheep at dawn, I found that they were not where I had left them at dusk, although I soon located them, huddled together in the shelter of a swale. All was well, so I left them with their guardian dogs to graze. Within a few hours, the herd wandered over to my camp, bedding in the brush above it, reposing in the sunshine, for a midmorning rest. The ewes are heavy with pregnancy, and lambing could begin at any time, although their official due date isn't for a few more days.

The wind blustered for most of the day, and the herd grazed in gullies and washes that offered protection from the gales. The range is covered with low vegetation that is high in nutrition but small in size due to the harsh climate. Jim tells me the low sagebrush the sheep currently seem to favor has a lemony flavor and is a rhizome, meaning it grows thick stems both below and above the ground. I drove around exploring the pasture, following the herd. I hiked the narrow passage between two slopes, following behind a small group of ewes to a grassy knoll, from which gurgled forth a spring of cold, clear water in a space the size of a washbasin.

With the blustery weather, there wasn't much avian activity, although I twice noticed the hardy little kestrel crisscrossing the brush in front of my camp, hunting fast and low to the ground. Its presence gives me joy, for this fierce little falcon is a species I much admire.

Late in the afternoon, Jim arrived to deliver supplies. It was wonderful to see him, but I fear he'll soon be run ragged with his job, taking care of home, and ferrying supplies to me once or twice a week. He restocked my water supply (scolding me for watering the dogs from my supply rather than from nature's offerings), delivered groceries and books, and helped insulate a vent in my camp that allowed the gusting wind to enter. His hour-long presence was welcome, but so short. He is worrying less, admires my undertaking, and admits to being a little envious of my life on the range. But it's because of his support that I'm able to be here, and I look forward to sharing the adventure with him.

As the sheep made their last grazing swath through the hills before nightfall, I watched their guardian dogs spread out around them. The dogs, each on separate routes, were hunting and exploring, disappearing into tall brush with their noses to the ground, digging in burrows, urine-marking where other predators had marked, and rolling on their backs, soaking up the smells that lingered on the ground. I was surprised when I saw Rena, a spayed female, urine-mark over a golden eagle's whitewash. She frequently urinates over coyote scat or marks, but the focus on an eagle's discharge was novel.

Rant postured at the summit of the tallest hill, the breeze rippling his neck ruff, his mid-docked tail erect, and emitted a few *woof, woof* calls into the valley below. He then dropped down into a natural duct, following its earthen flow to a small shelf in the hillside. Watching him from afar through binoculars, I could see his tail wag as he slapped one big front paw into a spot before him, a satisfying splash of water his reward. He'd found a seep and was amused with the discovery. Attracted by his antics, Rena joined Rant in inspecting the new water source. I left the dogs to their explorations and returned to camp.

Our livestock protection dogs are such an important part of our lives, it surprises me to learn that most people aren't aware of the vital role these animals play in successful livestock operations around the globe. They are our primary method of controlling predators.

Rant sits atop a hill, watching over the herd and the landscape below.

Livestock protection dogs are generally massive animals weighing one hundred pounds or more, with a natural guardian instinct. They can guard everything from flocks of domestic chickens and turkeys to herds of domestic sheep, cattle, and horses. In their countries of origin across Asia and Europe, the dogs have been used to guard livestock for not just hundreds but *thousands* of years.

Although guardian dogs have been used around the world for eons in primitive methods of livestock production, it's really only been in the last forty or so years that such dogs have been put to work in the United States in a systematic way. Their use here came about as a result of necessity. In 1972 the use of poisons to control predators (predacides) was banned on public lands in the West by presidential executive order, so domestic sheep producers needed to find an effective method of predator control to take their place. With passage of the Endangered Species Act a year later, methods of predator control also had to be environmentally friendly and not likely to cause harm to endangered or sensitive wildlife species. Livestock protection dogs were the answer.

Government agencies and universities in the United States worked together to begin importing livestock guardian dogs and placing them on ranches and farms across America. Livestock guardian dogs that had worked in the Pyrenees Mountains of France and Spain, the Anatolian Mountains of Turkey, and the steppes of Central Asia were eventually brought to the United States.

There are trade-offs to using guardian dogs. It means disallowing the use of snares, traps, or poisons within the dogs' range, because these methods of predator control could also kill or injure the dogs. (Although predator poisons had been banned from use on public lands, certain poisons remain available for use on private property.)

Just the presence of a couple of massive dogs with deep, booming barks charging forward is enough to deter many predators from trying to enter a herd to kill sheep. The dogs will keep their bodies between the predator and their herd, and will try to appear as large and aggressive as possible, with hackles up and tails held high. If the predator attempts to enter the herd, the dogs will physically attack the intruder, forcing it to flee or fight. Most predators will run away. Our dogs kill coyotes, but we've had guardians severely injured in combat with large predators. Some have been killed while protecting their herds. Wolves and bears are dangerous challengers.

Overall, livestock protection dogs have allowed many western sheep producers to stay in business by substantially reducing the amount of predation on domestic sheep herds. That's an impressive undertaking given that predator populations have expanded their ranges and increased in numbers at the same time. There are thousands of guardian dogs working on western rangelands, and those of us who are blessed by the pleasure of living and working with these animals can't imagine our part of the world without them.

The wind stopped just before dark, and the night was remarkably quiet, with no disturbance from coyotes. The sheep bedded in the brush of a hill nearby my camp, with Luv's Girl in their midst, while the other two guardian dogs served as silent sentinels on adjacent hills.

It's nine degrees this morning, cold and calm. When I went out for the first check of the sheep at dawn, they were still bedded. Within the hour, the herd had grazed its way to my camp, surrounding it as they lingered in the first rays of sunshine on my hillside. After putting away my bedding, cooking breakfast, and cleaning up, I looked out to find only one guardian dog in sight of the herd. Normally this isn't any reason for concern, but as lambing approaches, I take special note of the dogs' positions. When a ewe goes into labor, she'll either go off by herself or remain behind as the herd moves off to graze. Most of the time, a livestock guardian dog will stay with the ewe as she lambs, lying nearby, deliberately appearing unthreatening to the ewe, but posing a mighty obstacle to any that would disturb the birthing.

I was just cresting the hilltop to scan for the dogs and any isolated sheep when I came across a large cock sage grouse. The grouse did not seem particularly surprised by my sudden presence, although we paused to inspect each other before continuing about our business. Not glimpsing any errant animals from the hilltop, I went back to camp, where I spotted the dogs as they sat up to reveal themselves, wagging their tails in the thick brush above the sheep. From their vantages, the dogs could see the herd, but remain unseen themselves. Good guardians.

The forecast is for snow today, but the morning is still, with the sunshine taking the edge off the chill. It is so quiet that the jets crossing the sky tens of thousands of feet overhead seem to roar in disturbance.

As the day proceeds, the sheep are reluctant to wander far. More of the ewes are becoming ungainly, waddling with large bellies, heavy in pregnancy with multiple babes. Most range ewes produce single lambs with their first pregnancies, and twins thereafter, although triplets are not uncommon.

These ewes graze and rest in bountiful proportions. They are Rambouillet ewes, their fine-wool fleeces sheared from their bodies just a few weeks prior. Originating in France, the Rambouillet is a dual-purpose breed, producing both meat and wool, and is well suited to the western range. Their hot, pregnant bodies seem to thrive in the nippy Wyoming spring temperatures.

The ravens make frequent appearances, flying in low over the herd, harassing the resting ewes by landing on the ground next to them. The dogs quickly set the birds back into the air, but the ravens still worry the sheep.

Ravens are dangerous predators on a lambing ground, pecking on a ewe's backside as she strains in labor, or gouging the eyes of a newborn lamb before it can stand. When a raven lands on the ground next to a ewe and newborn, it may just be seeking to grab the afterbirth, but there is no way to predict their intentions, so ravens simply can't be tolerated on our lambing grounds, and the dogs are encouraged to ward them off.

Ravens have lived in association with humans for thousands of years, and have been so successful that they have become pests in some areas, preying on young livestock and crops, as well as displacing sensitive wildlife species, negatively impacting sage grouse chick-production in some areas.

An adult raven is a big, glossy-black bird with a thick beak, weighing more than three pounds, and over two foot in length with its wedge-shaped tail. These birds can live for four decades, and are believed to be highly intelligent, with advanced problem-solving skills. They seem to be very playful and make a wide range of sounds, including mimicking sounds they hear.

Bernd Heinrich's 1999 *Mind of the Raven* includes a list of both intelligent and strange "wolf-bird" behaviors, such as "ravens hanging by their feet, sliding in snow, snow-bathing, aerial bathing, flying upside down, doing barrel-rolls, social flying, and using objects to displace gulls from nests, using rocks in nest defense." Other reported behaviors include carrying food in the foot rather than the bill, foot pad-

Ravens are fascinating birds, but they pose a serious threat
to newborn lambs.

dling, rolling on the ground to avoid a peregrine falcon, catching
doves in midair, and attacking reindeer.

Ravens are frequently associated with coyotes and wolves, scavenging on their kills. The ravens followed in one study found wolf kills
almost immediately. Ravens are known as kleptoparasites because of
their feeding strategy of frequently stealing food obtained by other
animals.

✧ ✧ ✧ ✧

I check the sheep every two hours during the day—sometimes more,
rarely less during this time of year, as we wait for lambing to begin.

Passing the time here is easy for me: watching the sheep, watching the weather, and watching the wildlife. When in a landscape so big and so open, watching consumes a great deal of time. In these days before the ewes give birth, I read and write. I take a bucket bath during the warm period of the afternoons, while the sheep rest, chewing their cud.

I feel like this camping existence is somewhat luxurious—in my camper I have a small propane wall heater and stovetop, so it's fairly warm, and I can heat coffee or water when needed. There is no running water or electricity, but I have candles, flashlights, and a few electronic devices that can be charged in the pickup truck. I have various firearms tucked into handy places, and I am comfortable using all of them.

Rant barked outside my camp today, alerting me to the presence of a pickup truck on a butte three miles away. Like Rant, I find the unexpected presence of other people alarming, and was relieved when the truck disappeared into the distance. I'm not ready to share my solitude yet, with anyone except my beloved Jim.

My camp is comfortable, and the scenery outside my door is breathtaking. Brushing my teeth in the cool morning air is refreshing, and rolling frozen deodorant under my arms invigorating. I have a custom-made portable toilet, which I carry around until I find the view I want to contemplate. The toilet is made from an old molasses tub; Jim cut out the bottom and installed a toilet seat. I throw another old tub on top for storage, and no one is the wiser as to the contraption's purpose.

Overleaf: My portable toilet never lacks a beautiful view.

✧ ✧ ✧ ✧

The sheep herd arrived at my camp about fifteen minutes before the snowstorm hit. As a beautiful day drew to an end, the wind once again started to blow, bringing with it the snow I had watched falling in the higher elevations most of the afternoon. The storm was a blue-hued wall that crept across the sagebrush steppe, gobbling the landscape as it moved so that familiar features could no longer be demarcated. I had watched it traveling toward the camp as the day proceeded, as, evidently, had the sheep. We settled in to wait out the storm.

The weather wasn't too discomforting, initially. But long after the sun set, the gentle flakes riding on a light breeze developed into gusting wind-driven snow. Rena cried at the door to the camp a little after 1 A.M., begging to gain entrance. I had heard the guardian dogs and coyotes threatening each other before the gales began, and quickly let the guardian in, to rest and thaw. The wind blew the sheep from above my camp to just below it, on the side of a wide draw. Unfortunately, this was closer to the direction the coyote calling originated, so Rant and Luv's Girl were frantic during the night, racing back and forth barking their warnings into the raging wind.

By dawn, the dogs were exhausted and the sheep looked miserable, huddled together, their backs humped from the chill. The wind continued to blow, so after checking on the herd I returned to camp to fix breakfast and wait out the wind. Shortly after breakfast, as I sat in the truck listening to the news on the radio, the wind calmed and the sheep began to rise and stretch. The morning sunshine reflecting off the blanket of white covering the landscape was blindingly bright, and the sheep basked in its warmth.

According to the news, every interstate highway in Wyoming was closed due to treacherous driving conditions caused by the storm. I was thankful that all was well in my little corner of the world. The storm might have made things uncomfortable for a while, but it had not proved deadly for any of the animals. Tomorrow is our due date for lambing to start, and changes in the weather can initiate labor, so I was relieved no ewes had lambed during those precarious nighttime hours.

Leaving Rena to the warmth of my camp, I drove around the edge of the pasture, bumping down a two-track trail, the truck tires throwing up mud and snow as I proceeded. Looking for traces of animal activity in the new snow, I soon came across tracks that told a dramatic story. Smudge marks, chaotic impressions in an otherwise unmarred slate of white, revealed a battle that ended near the fence line of rusted barbed wire. The jackrabbit had ventured out to forage, digging through the snow to nibble grass and brush, only to see a dark shape approaching overhead. The jack ran, making frantic leaps, evasive dodges to the left and right, blasting at full speed toward the safety of the fence. With any luck, the hungry eagle above would smash to its death in the wire, and the jack would go back to its meal.

But luck today would be with the eagle. Powerful wings pumped the raptor body forward, as dagger-like talons reached down to pluck life from the jack. The bird came to rest on the jack's body, a fluff of downy fur covering the eagle's only meal of the day. The bird's wingtips left indentations in the powdery white covering the earth, as the raptor again rose from the ground.

The jack and the eagle, two species that live in close association, are typical wild creatures in that neither lives to old age. Wild animals rarely do.

Life and death in the wild are interconnected, daily experiences. The death of the jack is not to be mourned, as the death provides continued life for the magnificent golden raptor. The cycle continues, in the biting cold of winter, and in the warmth of a spring sunrise.

The basin's jackrabbits aren't actually rabbits but members of the hare family, related to snowshoe hares. Hares are born open-eyed and furred, while rabbits are born naked, with closed eyes. Hares live above ground in small depressions, while rabbits live in underground burrows.

Jackrabbits live in the same habitats year-round, but move to open grazing areas at night from their shrub-covered daytime hiding places. Eight jackrabbits can consume as much food as one domestic sheep, with each jack eating up to a pound of green vegetation per

A jackrabbit uses its winter camouflage to hide in the snow.

day. Jackrabbit populations fluctuate, and when populations increase, droves of these hares can be seen.

Jackrabbits often become aggressive toward each other during breeding season, and when jacks concentrate into dense groups, boxing matches are frequent. Most of the time it's a female slapping a male, and since females are much larger in size than the males, it's entertaining to watch.

Years ago when there was a boom in the jack population in the West, jackrabbit drives would be conducted to control damage to grain fields, haystacks, and other stored forage. Hunters would spread out across a parcel of land, forcing the jacks to move in front of them, driving them into fenced traps for killing. The meat was usually donated to charities. One California drive netted six thousand jacks. Predation has a limited role in controlling jackrabbit populations, which tend to cycle through booms, with peaks and crashes.

When I drove back to camp, I could see Rena inside, lying on my bed, looking out the window. Apparently she was taking an extended break. Luv's Girl was outside, sitting in the sun and using the camp as her backdrop. Rant was curled up out in the snowy sagebrush, oh so stiff and weary. I had tried to get him to step into the warmth of a small stock trailer parked in camp, but he had refused.

Rant is an Aziat, or Central Asian Ovcharka, the runt of a litter bred in the United States by a Russian breeder. It is this type of dog that the Kuchi use with their herds, and that are used in organized dogfights in Afghanistan to test their suitability for challenging wolves. He was brought here to the western range to be raised to face our wolves. The same type of dog is used to guard livestock from wolves throughout Central Asia, although the name of the breed varies: Aziat in Russia, Alabai or Kopek or Volkodav ("wolf killer") in Turkmenistan, and Tobet in Kazakhstan, but they all fall into the Ovcharka group.

Two years ago, when my Basque sheepman friend Pete and I purchased four of these Aziat pups, we were told the pedigree six generations back: In the early 1990s, an adult male was exported from Turkmenistan to Russia and bred there to a dam that had been purchased as a pup from a herder in Tajikistan. The adult male, Gjock, was tried as a fighting dog in Turkmenistan, but apparently did not show much promise. A few years later, these dogs, with some of their progeny, were imported to the United States. I named the male pups Turk and Rant, and the females Helga and Vega. The littermates are the first of their kind being used in range-sheep operations in western Wyoming.

I raise livestock protection dog pups in partnership with Pete, who owns a large migratory range-sheep outfit and has upwards of twenty guard dogs working with his herds at any one time. We generally raise a litter a year, which means that at the home ranch, I am often living with puppies. I raise the pups for Pete and other sheep producers in this region because our small ranch provides a good environment for the pups to bond with young lambs, have their first predator encounters, and prepare to go on the migratory sheep trail.

In this realm of migratory livestock production, the toughest stud dogs win breeding rights to females, although every now and then Pete and I will handpick dogs for breeding. Once the female is pregnant, the male goes back to the sheep trail, while the female hangs out with my sheep, taking it easy. Pete calls it guardian-dog vacation.

The dogs are challenged by coyotes every day (and now and then by a mountain lion, bear, or wolf), and we have dead coyotes in our sheep pastures on a regular basis. We call coyote and red fox carcasses "puppy chewies" because they are scattered around puppy territory every summer. Most pups have their first altercation—which makes them mad enough to make their first kill—before they lose their puppy teeth, which happens when they are about four or five months old. From then on, they are pups with a mission.

Just as wolves have been persecuted throughout the world, and wolf populations threatened with extinction in some countries, the guardian dogs that protect livestock from wolf predation have declined as well. Without pressure from large carnivores, and with livestock herds decreasing worldwide, use of these dogs has fallen off to the extent that there are now recovery programs in place to get the dogs back onto their historic landscapes along with expanding large-carnivore populations in their countries of origin.

The spread of communism throughout Central Asia brought with it an active campaign to rid entire regions of its free peoples—the nomadic livestock cultures. Livestock and their guardian dogs were killed or collectivized, and their nomadic herders and families were taken from the land. When the herders became villagers, the cultures lost their old traditions.

In the 1930s, demand for dog skins resulted in the destruction of the largest dogs available, while rabies campaigns called for wholesale extermination of all dogs in certain regions, including livestock guardian dogs. Later, intermixing of dog breeds and outbreaks of various dog diseases combined to take a toll on native dog populations. The loss of interest in livestock husbandry, as well as a decline in predator populations as a result of human persecution, also played a role in the reduction of working guardian dogs. Recent interest in national dog breeds has resulted in a greater demand for dogs in the pet trade than as working animals, and some livestock guardian dogs are now being used and bred for dogfighting rather than guarding herds. Livestock guardian dogs actively working to protect herds are a precious resource, no matter where they are located.

Kazakhstan has the highest density of wolves in the world, and guardian dogs are the only reliable form of protection from predation there. Ovcharkas, called Tobets in Kazakhstan, are the breed of choice.

Kazakhstan also finds itself working to encourage and rebuild its transhumance livestock-production system, which was once the basis of Kazakh culture. As it did throughout the region, Russian occupation of Kazakhstan dismantled the transhumance system in favor of collectivized agriculture, with state- or collective-owned farms keeping large numbers of animals on supplied supplemental feed. The country is now faced with vastly underutilized grazing range, but heavily overgrazed areas near towns. With the realization that supporting infrastructure (services, trailing routes, and water supplies) has been depleted or no longer exists, Kazakhstan officials are working to create a new program of transhumance, since it cannot simply return to the old system.

Kazakhstan is not alone in its efforts. Central Asia's rangelands are the world's largest continuous area of grazed land, encompassing more than 640 million acres. The regional move from transhumance to the creation of permanent pastures has resulted in overall degradation, with overgrazing in permanent pastures, and underutilization in more remote regions causing a buildup of soil crust, reduced water absorption, and replacement of valuable pasture flora with moss and lichens. Work is now under way to restore rotational grazing patterns associated with the Central Asian tradition of transhumance herding.

Some who profess to be concerned with nature and all that is natural take the view that humankind is somehow not part of the natural equation. But mankind is integral to the wholeness of nature. We're part of nature, not outside it as mere observers. It's the human aspect of nature that I fear is in the process of being lost, and it's happening worldwide. The practice of transhumance involves man and beast living together on the land, moving together with the seasons, responding to natural conditions. It involves becoming a part of nature.

Transhumance is most visible to me, where I live, when I see domestic sheep herds on open rangelands. The herds slowly move with the seasons, wintering on the windblown sage lands near the Colorado border, moving north as the days get longer. They arrive in western Wyoming's Farson country by early May, pausing on their journey to give birth to bright white lambs before continuing to graze their way into the Wind River Range, reaching high-elevation meadows in July, and finally being chased back to lower country by September snows. Sheepherders live with the sheep, walking among them by day, hearing those small teeth nibble and clip the tasty new vegetative growth, watching little tufts of dirt rise into the air as hooves strike the ground as the sheep move as one. Herders gently lend a hand to a ewe straining in the process of birthing, and are comforted as they listen to soft sheep sounds in the darkness of night in an archaic camp.

The movement of the sheep, and their human herders, is as natural as the movement of the wildlife herds that follow the same path. The nomadic herders know much about nature because they are a part of it.

Transhumance is agriculture in its most natural form. It is food production without chemicals and captivity, in a pristine landscape. If we lose the practice of transhumance, we will have lost a vital component of the natural state of humankind.

Migrating with the seasons in response to food availability is a natural occurrence that has taken place for millions of years. Renowned Spanish naturalist Jesus Garzón reports that for the last five million years, Iberian wildlife and herbivores have migrated from lowland valleys in winter to summer grazing high in the mountains, and that eight thousand years ago, during the Neolithic period, the shepherds who domesticated wild game continued using these same migration routes. Eventually the network of routes throughout Spain was used for cattle droving and sheep herding, and the first settlements and villages were located along these routes. Garzón maintains that those who seek to exclude man from the natural world are mistaken—man is an essential part of nature, and the natural community has evolved with man's influence. While some governments are seeking to install "greenways" and "migration corridors," those with transhumance systems already have these areas in place, and their continued use by pastoralists and livestock will help to maintain their existence.

As evening neared, I drove to the top of the hill behind my camp to watch the sheep moving toward me, grazing as they navigated the tall sagebrush along the neighboring hill, a scattering of snow lingering on the ground. A single raven flew above the herd, then turned and headed toward it; flying menacingly just above the ewe's heads, the bird actually managed to turn the herd back in the direction from which it had come. I was flabbergasted that one raven could be so bold. If a single bird could have that effect on the entire herd, what might happen when a ewe lays down to labor?

As I pondered this question, a pickup truck appeared in the distance. I trained my binoculars on the object and had just ascertained its identity when my cell phone rang. It was friend Pete and his Nepalese foreman Prem, advising me that they were about to stop in for a quick visit. We sat on the hillside in our trucks as the temperature dropped, talking about the sheep, the guardian dogs and our predator encounters, the forage available for the sheep, the snowstorm, and what water sources we were utilizing. When we turned to go our separate ways, the sun was beginning to slip under the western horizon, and as we said our goodnights, our words were accentuated by small puffs of condensation as our warm breaths met the cold night air.

CHAPTER 2

settling in

◇ ◇ ◇

Dawn reveals a silver-coated landscape, frost covering every conceivable surface, and as the sun begins its slow rise over the Wind River Mountains, the frost quickly recedes, leaving only sparkling droplets of moisture in its wake. It was eleven degrees when I made the first check of the herd, on this date we are due to being lambing. The sheep were still contentedly bedded, so I left them to their rest.

I stand outside my camp and gaze at the mountains before me, trying to name the peaks and drainages up and down the range. As I gaze to the north, my thoughts go to the cattle ranches nestled into the upper valley, and the families that use the land. There are about a dozen family ranches involved in the Green River Drift, a long-distance migration of cattle from western Wyoming's desert grazing allotments into the mountains of the Upper Green River region, onto the largest cattle allotment in the National Forest System. Farther down the mountain range, Pete's French-Basque family summers thousands of domestic sheep high in the lush meadows of the Wind River Mountains before trailing the flocks more than 150 miles to winter in the windswept desert near Wyoming's border with Colorado.

Here in the West, the land along waterways is mostly privately held, with the majority of the surrounding lands owned by the public and administered by the federal government. The Bureau of Land Management is responsible for much of the desert and sagebrush lands of the West, while the US Forest Service manages the high country, the mountains and wilderness.

With so little moisture in the arid West, it takes many acres of land

---

Overleaf: The herd of pregnant ewes paws fresh snow aside to find forage.

to support a livestock outfit and allow it to be profitable. Since there is so little private land, public lands are used for part of the year. It's this combination of land ownership that allows for livestock production on the western range. An action that weakens one segment can lead to instability for an entire ranch outfit.

Like the big-game herds that live alongside domestic herds, range livestock move with the seasons. In general, livestock are wintered on private property, spend the spring on BLM lands, and, as the snow melts in the high country, move onto Forest Service lands for summer and fall. As winter storms threaten, livestock and wildlife both begin moving back to the lower country.

The private property along waterways is used to grow native hay and alfalfa through flood-irrigation systems. These crops grow while the livestock herds are on public land, are harvested before they return, and fed to the cattle and sheep during the winter months. Various species of wildlife live alongside livestock throughout the year.

Some of the livestock that move in this seasonal grazing pattern make relatively short passages; other herds make much longer journeys. Some are trucked and some are trailed. The distance may be 30 miles or it may be 130 miles.

As a sheep herd moves across the range, local plant seeds are deposited in their wool and in their hooves, and these seeds are transported to other areas along the transhumance route, promoting genetic diversity in floral species, which in turn promotes insect diversity, which promotes a diversity of bird life, and on up the natural chain. The sheep's hooves break up the soil surface, and the sheep's dung fertilizes the soil, promoting vegetative growth. One German experiment found the seeds of eighty plant species in one sheep fleece.

If grazing is abandoned, larger, more competitive grass species take over, stifling the smaller and less competitive species. Grazing promotes diversity by providing openings and clearings in brush, so that small mammals like voles and rabbits may thrive, which in turn are prey for a variety of predators. When the land grows truly "wild," its plant diversity declines as aggressive species choke out other growth, and animal diversity thus declines as well. Lands can convert to scrub and trees, with fuel buildups setting the stage for catastrophe. The loss of transhumance can result in wildfires, and the loss of regeneration of native trees, and the cascade effect of local bird extinctions, according to the Spanish naturalist Jesus Garzón.

Spain's rich and ancient history with transhumance shows that at one point in time, shepherds were highly regarded and granted privileges not available to others. The Spanish king Alfonso the Wise authorized transhumance and declared official migratory trails in 1273. Shepherds were given two general directives: do not traverse cornfields, hayfields, or vineyards; and walk *como mujer hilando,* or slowly, in the manner of a woman spinning wool to pass the time as she follows the flock. The shepherd could carry a firearm to protect the flock, and was exempt from military service. Even if accused of a crime, the shepherd could not be removed from the flock for trial because that would leave the sheep untended.

This traditional way of life, practiced over thousands of years, gradually declined after the installation of a rail system, and many segments of the long-distance transhumance network became paved for vehicles and transport.

Garzón has been praised for his work in reestablishing transhumance in Spain, which is said to have saved the mountains from

abandonment. Ghost villages are reawakening along historic transhumance routes, and local people are returning to their ancestral
homes in the mountains.

Spain now uses transhumance as a tool for nature conservation,
working over the last twenty years or so to reestablish the country's
network of historic migration routes and practices. Young shepherds
are being trained on the routes in coordination with their home
farms. Local villages and towns host celebrations and fairs for the arrival of the trailing animals.

More than one million cattle are involved in transhumance movements in Spain, and conservationists hope to increase that number,
with the installation of water sources along the routes and other
measures. Many wildlife species also follow these routes, as they have
for eons, and the renewal of transhumance benefits them as well.

Germany has initiated a program in which drover routes used in
transhumance are also used to facilitate the exchange of individuals
of rare wildlife species between populations, reducing inbreeding
and reestablishing extinct populations. Germans expect to use transhumance to mitigate the negative effects of climate change that
would reduce natural diversity.

As I watch ranches in the western United States teetering on the
edge of profitability, coping with natural elements to extract a living
from this wild landscape, it pains me to see the political forces lined
up to drive us away. The environmental/preservationist push toward
some kind of unrealizable pre-Columbian utopia, combined with a
government bureaucracy that seeks complete control of the landscape, constitutes an assault on the very viability of primitive agriculture on the western range—when the loss of livestock grazing would

be disastrous for both local ecosystems and communities. The land needs ranchers, just as ranchers need the land.

After the cold start to the day, the temperature reached the midthirties, and all the regional animal life seemed to enjoy the relatively mild weather, with its slight breezes and patchy clouds. At an elevation this high (about 7,500 feet), cloudy days provide for visual drama, with darkness followed by startling brightness as the skies change overhead. The sheep moved in a slow, circular pattern throughout the day, arriving at my hillside camp in early afternoon. I'm not sure if it was the walk uphill or the pregnancy hormones raising their body temperatures, but for whatever reason, the girls came to a standstill around the camp, softly panting. I squatted down on the ground to be at their level, and one young ewe came over to sniff my mouth, as sheep tend to do to each other. Surely the smell of my fruit, bread, and cheese lunch was incomparable to the heady onion smell emanating from the ewe's mouth. Several other ewes approached, allowing me to sniff their noses and rub their chests. Ah, such sweet sheep.

Our sheep may have a uniform look, but they have distinct personalities. One of our girls is named Assistant Sheep, because often when I'm engaged in chores or outside work she follows alongside as if she's my helper, sticking her nose into everything.

River is a big sweet ewe that Cass raised on a bottle. She was rescued from drowning in the river when she was about two days old.

Wrinkle Nose is a nice older ewe. That is, she's nice right up until the time she lambs, when she turns into a vicious monster, suspecting everyone and everything of being out to steal her new baby. She's butted me in the butt before, for touching her lamb, even though I'm her favorite person. She's a very protective mother.

The lambs need good mothers or they'd never survive. They are born tiny, with long, shaky legs; they look like they're wearing a thin white coat of skin pulled over a bundle of bones. But they get up within minutes and start dancing around with the ewes, trying to find the milk bag to nurse while their mom licks them off and tries to get them clean. Our fat ewes give birth to lambs that can stand cold temperatures at birth, their rich milk providing plenty of energy for the lambs to stay warm and thrive even in cold, snowy weather. Most of our ewes give birth to twins, and a few to triplets. That's fine, but I don't think most ewes can count past two, so I am usually called upon to help raise the extras.

Lambs like to cuddle with their moms and sometimes they stand on top of their mothers while the mothers are lying down trying to rest. Some lambs will curl up and sleep on top of their moms, in that soft wool bed. I know how comfortable that is, because there are a few ewes that will let me lay my head on their backs while they rest during the day. I've nearly fallen asleep like that, but not quite, because when sheep lie around resting, they chew their cuds. That means every few minutes they make a little hiccup as they bring the cud into their mouths. The action makes your head bounce if you are trying to take a nap. I'm betting there aren't too many people who know that bit of trivia, but plenty of sheepmen do.

With the quelling of the wind, the birds are back above us. As I visited with the ewes, our neighborhood kestrel hovered in the foreground, hunting in the sagebrush below. I followed the ewes along the

hill and toward Coyote Rocks, to see a pair of golden eagles flying together, soaring high above the herd, the snowy mountains their backdrop.

A group of seven ravens flew near the sheep herd, and several of
them broke off to land amid the ewes, disturbing them and making
them run. Pete had told me about a group of ravens that had been attacking newborn calves at a ranch not too distant, so I fear the ravens
and I are about to have a falling out. Ravens are federally protected
under the Migratory Bird Treaty Act. When livestock producers incur
damages from these birds, they cannot take action themselves but
must call in federal wildlife officials for relief. I intend to make that
call soon, because such aggressive behavior toward adult ewes can
only bode ill for newborn lambs.

The Green River basin is recovering from nearly a decade of drought,
and our snowpack this winter was scant, but drought may not be as
critical as another threat we face: receding glaciers.

The Wind River Mountains are home to sixty-three glaciers covering seventeen square miles, including seven of the ten largest glaciers
in the Rocky Mountains. These natural formations are popular for fish-
ing, mountain climbing, and backpacking, but more importantly, they
serve as water-storage reservoirs, contributing to downstream flow in
late summer and fall.

In the late 1980s researchers at the University of Wyoming examined the 1.4-square-mile Gannett Glacier and the 1.2-square-mile Dinwoody Glacier and estimated that the Gannett had lost 61 feet of
depth since 1958, while the depth loss due to melt was 77 feet at

Dinwoody during the same time period. The water-equivalent loss was 48,000 acre-feet at Gannett and 52,000 acre-feet at Dinwoody. An acre-foot is the volume of water needed to cover one acre of land up to a depth of one foot.

Researchers calculated that the area covered by the glaciers declined 36 percent from 1950 to 1999, a period of forty-nine years, but the most loss, at 25 percent, was more recent (from 1989 to 1999). That's an alarming rate, because without late-season water flows from the mountains, the ability to flood-irrigate to provide winter forage for domestic stock, as well as lush riparian habitat for wildlife, will decline.

In 2002 US Geological Survey scientists sampled glacial ice cores in the Wind Rivers, and determined that the average air temperature in the high elevations may have increased by more than six degrees in the preceding five years.

Forty percent of the world's population depends on or is influenced by water from rivers that originate on the Tibetan plateau. The Chinese government has instituted a "western development" policy that seeks to conserve the Tibetan grasslands by forced relocation of its nomadic herders and their livestock off traditional grazing lands, and halting grazing in the region for a ten-year period to repair any degradation caused by overgrazing in the past. Of course, this reasoning fails to recognize that the plateau has evolved with grazing as a primary component, and the adverse effects of the woven-wire fences that are being erected over vast regions will eventually become evident. Halting transhumance in favor of permanent pastures often results in ecological and economic decline. Government officials hope to move at least one hundred thousand people from their nomadic existence in the Sanjiangyuan region and place them into specially constructed "resettlement villages," with such a move based on an assumption that urbanization is preferable to pastoralism. What is happening on the Tibetan plateau is simply heartbreaking, and is reminiscent of what is happening to public-lands livestock grazing in the western United States as ranchers are forced off the range.

Ranchers in the American West face forced closure of grazing allotments as preservationists call for larger and larger wildlife populations, and proclaim their unwillingness to share public range with private enterprise. The federal bureaucracy governing the system creates mounds of regulations for compliance, failing to recognize the reality of nature and its ever-changing conditions. It saddens me to see the United States actively moving toward systems that we have seen fail throughout the world, as livestock raisers are taken from the land.

A few days later, I awoke in the early-morning darkness to the soothing sound of raindrops falling on the roof of the camp. I crawled out of my warm sleeping bag and started the coffee heating on the stove while I dressed, savoring the sound as the light drizzle continued. A quick trip outside revealed that the sheep were still bedded in a stand of tall sagebrush, so I left them to their rest and returned to camp to wait for the sun to rise.

Although the ewes are now overdue, it's not of concern since we're used to about a 10-day variation before lambing begins each year. Yesterday afternoon's nearly fifty-degree temperatures resulted in the sheep spending most of the day lounging on hillsides, chewing their cuds and panting from the heat of their pregnant bodies. Cass, just home from his freshman year in college, had agreed to take my place in camp the night before so that I could go home and attend to personal and business matters that had accumulated during the week of my absence. I managed to take both a bubble bath and a shower in the short time I was home, apparently making up for all those bucket baths during the week in camp. Jim helped me load my supplies into the truck, and next we tackled the big job I'd been anxious about— getting my guardian burros to camp. I had hated to be without the pair the previous week, and I was looking forward to their presence on the range, knowing they would provide some needed relief for the exhausted dogs.

Bill and Hillary are in their midteens, born wild on the range in Nevada, rounded up by federal officials, and adopted by a Montana sheepman (who named them). When he passed away and the ranch and all its livestock were sold, Cass and I made the journey to Montana to purchase the burros from his widow. Bill and Hillary are gentle souls, more similar in behavior to large dogs than to horses, rather slow-moving thinkers not prone to hysteria, and I love them dearly.

Wild donkeys, or burros, have a natural aversion to members of the canine family and have been used to protect livestock in Africa for centuries, although the practice is relatively new to North America. Our burros have proven to be great guardians to the herd. Their in-stinctive dislike for canines includes not just coyotes but dogs as well. The process of introducing a new livestock protection dog to the bur-ros is slow going, and must be well supervised to ensure the safety of

Our loyal burros, Bill and Hillary, join their herd on the open range.

the dogs. Our burros quickly learn that the dogs have the same goal of protecting the sheep, but they have never fully trusted our herding dogs.

The burros will attempt to run down and attack any strange canine, striking with their front hooves, kicking with their hind hooves, and trying to bite the animal. We believe that the visible presence of large animals within our sheep herd also serves as a deterrent to predators sizing up the possibility of making a successful attack.

When we had penned the sheep for transport to the range, Bill and

Hillary had watched from nearby—close enough to see the goings-on but unwilling to take part. We had left them free in the home pasture for the week, along with a young burro, Roo. The evening I returned home, I lured all three burros into the pen with the promise of graham crackers from my coat pockets. After all else was readied for the trip back to camp the next morning, I placed halters and lead ropes on the two older burros, and Jim trimmed Hillary's hooves before we loaded the two into the stock trailer. Amid all the activity, the burros were sweating and even shivering in anxiety, but nonetheless did everything we asked with patient acceptance. Roo would be turned loose in the home pasture to watch over the ram herd, but not before Jim had given her some special attention.

It was a long hour's drive to get the burros to the sheep herd, but when we arrived, Jim slipped off their halters and they jumped out of the trailer, eyeing the sheep in the valley below. The burros slowly began making their way in that direction, careful not to scare their charges. Later in the afternoon I checked on them to see if they were enjoying their freedom, and they both walked up to me for attention and were rewarded with half of a bagel that happened to be waiting in my coat pocket.

After Jim and Cass had left for home, everything was so peaceful I decided an afternoon nap was in order. I drove one last check around the sheep as they grazed below Coyote Rocks, spotting Rena in my rearview mirror up on the rocks as I returned to camp.

An hour later I startled awake, afraid I had slept too long. I headed for the sheep herd and found all well there, the burros amid the bunch. I counted dogs as I went, and soon realized that Rena was nowhere to be found. I got on my dirt bike and quickly backtracked over the sheep's movements that day, thinking that perhaps a ewe was off by herself in labor, with Rena attending. No such luck—the sheep were all together, and no sign of Rena. As I rode the pasture's perimeter, my heart sank. I was soon beating myself up for not paying Rena more attention before my nap. I checked the reservoir, and the spring—nothing. Time was ticking by—soon I had searched for her for two full hours, and that meant she could have been gone for three hours already. She could have gone after a coyote, but wouldn't she be back by now?

Had the arrival of the burros, and Jim and Cass leaving again, presented too much disruption for Rena, prompting her to leave camp, perhaps to head for home? The big danger wasn't from any risk in the outdoors, but that she would be stolen. She is a beautiful, large, bright-white dog who is friendly and well mannered. Someone encountering her would be sorely tempted to keep her.

As I scoured the hills, valleys, and badlands through binoculars, my heart would quicken at a glimpse of white in the brush, only to become crestfallen as I realized I had mistaken a pronghorn antelope for our dear guardian.

I called Jim to alert him to Rena's absence and my concern, and he immediately jumped in the truck to head back toward camp, keeping a lookout along the way in case the dog had decided to head for home. Just as Jim was reaching the gate to the pasture, I saw a white form moving up the hillside toward camp. It was Rena! She was exhausted, filthy, footsore, and soaking wet. She had apparently gone after something (most likely a coyote) and had pursued it long enough that by the time she returned she was worn out, collapsing in an exhausted heap outside my camp door. I was thankful that four hours after her adventure began, she was safely back where she should be. Jim once again left for home, and I adjourned for bed, as exhausted as the dog.

I slept soundly, but my slumber was disturbed a few hours later when I heard Rena bark just behind the camp. It wasn't a distant-threat-warning kind of bark, or a making-noise-at-a-coyote bark, but a serious imminent-trouble bark. *Oh no.* Whatever it was, it was right outside my door. As I stuck my feet into my slippers and grabbed the flashlight to head out, I thought to myself, *This is a really bad idea,* but continued out into the night and around the side of the camp anyway, where the cause of the disturbance was immediately evident. The burros had decided to make a late-night visit, checking out the dog-food bowls, which Rena was busy defending. Relieved, I grabbed the bowls and threw them down inside the camp door as I jumped back into my sleeping bag.

Two hours after sunrise, the light drizzle changed to snow. I did another check of the herd and returned to camp, the truck spraying mud as I traveled. Rant stuck his head up from a stand of sagebrush to let me know he was in the area, and then disappeared back into the landscape. Rena insisted on bringing her dirty, wet, and weary body into my camp for a nap, while Abe and Luv's Girl slept outside. Luv's Girl had appeared in camp at morning's first light, leaving the resting herd in the care of its two burros. The dangers of the night had passed.

Our livestock protection dogs display a range of behavioral differences when it comes to guardian duties. Luv's Girl is always with the sheep, never venturing far, sleeping among them and moving with them as though she's part of the herd. When the herd enters a pen, she's with them, and when we shear, we have to move Luv's Girl out of the way. When we load sheep into a stock trailer, she cries at the door to the trailer, begging us to reconsider. When she comes to camp to

Luv's Girl, happily surrounded by her herd.

eat or take a break, it's only if the herd is otherwise guarded and nearby. She is calm and experienced, and she licks her sheep's noses as she rejoins them, demonstrating her affection in a physical way.

Rant is more reserved with the sheep, and being in close contact with them can make him nervous, as he has greater personal-space requirements than the other dogs. Rant is exceedingly powerful; his body is massive and muscular. There is no excess fat on his frame, despite constant access to food. He prefers to guard from a high spot nearby the herd, where he can see the surroundings and respond to threats. He does not lick or show affection to adult sheep, but he is very loving toward and possessive of baby lambs.

Rant is our youngest guardian dog, and he has the least amount of judgment when it comes to assessing threats. When Rant is presented with a young animal such as a lamb, guarding the vulnerable creature becomes all-consuming. He believes anything could be a threat to the baby, even the lamb's mother. He becomes overly excited and will stand guard over his charge, clacking his huge teeth together nervously. It is a terrifying show, but I am generally able to calm him with a soothing repetition of "Easy, easy." I hope that as he matures, he'll become more relaxed and better able to size up threats. But it's his high level of devotion that makes him an excellent guardian. The only way to stop him from defending a herd member would be if he were killed in battle. While other dogs might hesitate when faced with a serious threat, Rant is likely to rush in headlong. Aziats are most famous for their willingness and ability to challenge wolves, which is why we wanted this breed.

Here on the range, Rant displays the classic behavior of a guardian dog moving into an area and occupying the canid niche. Most nights he is vocal and active, loudly declaring his territory and running after coyotes to challenge them. He returns in the mornings weary from his nighttime activities, and can be seen throughout the day, rarely with the sheep, but patrolling the perimeter of the square-mile area where the sheep graze. He moves across the range slowly, inspecting animal burrows and urine-marking the territory, seeking cover in the brush to take naps. Jim caught Rant napping next to a Coyote Rocks den the other day. This is typical canine displacement behavior, where the dogs take over the coyotes' territory, attempting to push them out of the area.

Raising the litter of Aziat pups was an adventure in itself. Rant and his three siblings had been flown from the East Coast to our house in the Northern Rockies as soon as they were weaned. Rant, the runt, had barely survived the ordeal, but within a few days all four pups were recuperating nicely in a kennel behind my house. I had other livestock protection pups from a litter Pete had at his ranch, and a few orphan lambs, so the pups began the socialization process at a fairly young age. I also let the dogs into the house on occasion, reasoning that it was part of the training process: when we visited the veterinarian's office in town, the dogs would know how to behave inside a building. By the time the pups were about six months old, they were in the ninety-pound range, but still very much immature beasts—they were the "terrible twos" of the dog world, and as uncoordinated and gangly as pubescent boys.

Overleaf: This is coyote territory, but Rant will soon make it his.

One fall afternoon when the pups were adolescents provides an example. I use a hose to fill the stock water tank behind our house, and the cold of a fall night could result in the hose freezing. After a long trip to town, I let the dogs out of the kennel and got busy unloading groceries and doing other chores. The hose was frozen when I went to fill the water tank, so I coiled it and brought it into the house to thaw in a hot tub. I then took it back out, reattached it, ran it back to the tank, and filled the tank. I was in and out both the front and back doors repeatedly during this process.

It was a simple enough task, until the livestock guardian pups decided to help. That meant chasing the horses away from the stock tank—even though the tank's sole purpose is to water the horses; the dogs have their own tank in the kennel.

After getting the hose taken care of, I walked in the back door to find one of the littermates, the ninety-pound monster Helga, on one of my two leather couches in the living room, her mouth bleeding. She acted shy, as though she knew she had done something wrong, all tho while dripping blood all over the couch and throw pillows. I grabbed a kitchen towel and hurried toward her, which spooked her, so she leapt off the couch, flew across the room, and landed on the other couch, leaving a blood trail along the way.

Helga was embarrassed about the bleeding and didn't want me to touch her, but I was trying to minimize the damage to the house, so we obviously weren't on the same wavelength. I chased, she ran, blood flew. Rant came bolting through the front door to find out what the fuss was about, which then set Helga into another flight response. I grabbed a package of pastries from the top of the breadbox on the counter, flung open the back door, and hurled the package out the door, the guardian dogs quickly jumping out after them. I slammed the door after the hell hounds were outside.

I then backtracked and found blood on the outside of the front door where Helga had hit it with her nose to get it open. The best I can figure, she sufficiently harassed the horses at the stock tank that one of them finally had enough and kicked her in the mouth. As it turned out, there was no damage to her mouth or teeth; the blood came from a nick in her tongue. She'd come into the house seeking comfort, but once she got there she didn't want anyone to touch her.

As an added bonus, while I ran around cleaning the house, I found large chunks of raw sweet potatoes scattered in the living room, on the couch, and in the hall. I had just filled the vegetable basket on the kitchen sideboard with sweet potatoes when I returned home, and while I was outside, the monster pups decided to steal something—there were two potatoes gone from the basket. Guess they made good toys, but weren't actually worthy of ingesting. All this happened in a period of fifteen minutes.

A few days later, a neighbor stopped by the house to let me know she had spotted a lamb outside our boundary fence. It turns out I hadn't completely shut the front door when I went out to speak to the woman as she sat in her car. When I thanked her and turned to go back into the house, I saw several pairs of Cass's underwear scattered on the lawn. Helga had been busy, quietly walking back and forth in and out of the front door, taking things outside to play with. I picked up her "toys" and put them back in the laundry basket from where they had originated.

One morning I wanted to take a quick shower, so I locked the Aziat pups in the front yard, inside the confines of our wooden picket fence. While I was in the shower, I heard the dogs raising a ruckus, but by the time I could get out of the shower and look out the window, the pups had chomped a huge hole through the front fence. Whatever had prompted this activity was over with, but the hole and slivers of wood were very impressive.

All four Aziat pups took to an early liking to chasing down coyotes. The girls, Helga and Vega, developed a unique method, with Vega, the faster of the two, chasing the coyotes in the direction where Helga would be hiding, whereupon Helga would jump out and inflict the killing blow on the unsuspecting predator. They became a lethal pair.

We worried about a pack of coyotes getting one of the pups out alone and killing it, but these dogs were pros. We called them "coyote proof" by the time they weighed about thirty five pounds. Turk eventually became top dog in Pete's outfit, but when he matured, he became far more interested in breeding rights than staying with a single sheep herd. Being a guardian became somewhat secondary to his other duties.

As hardheaded as the day is long, Rena has always been an interesting animal to live with. As a pup, she was constantly picking fights with her siblings, and getting beat up for it because she was smaller. As she grew, she liked to stalk herding-dog Abe like she was a lion about to make a kill—very slowly, very intently, with intimidation.

One day when Rena was still a young pup, Luv's Girl killed a coyote in the sheep pasture, and the carcass was left in full view of the sheep pen. Rena saw it and became very alarmed.

After barking at the carcass from a distance, Rena finally decided it was time to check it out. Nearing the dead animal, her hackles went up and she slowed her pace. Rena walked stiff-legged to the carcass, emitting a low growl from deep within her chest. She cautiously stuck her nose out to sniff the still body, stalking around it in a circle while she convinced herself that the coyote was dead. At first Rena was scared, but it seemed the more convinced she was that the coyote was dead, the more wildly excited she became.

Rena's barks were furious as she approached closer, jumping back and forth around the coyote, tilting her head to threaten it at different angles and hopping forward to nip at the mane on the back of its neck. She'd get a mouthful of fur, then snarl and shake her head as if she were killing the beast. It was good practice for a young pup.

The dogs have involved us in some of their coyote adventures. One warm and snowy morning, Jim took Rena over to our winter sheep pasture so he could check on the livestock and fill the water tank. Rena soon barked frantically from behind the corral, and then came running to get Jim. He grabbed a gun and man-and-dog team went hunting after a pair of coyotes. Jim shot once and missed. Rena gave chase, trying to bite the coyote in front of her while the second coyote tried to bite her from behind. She was pretty proud of herself, and seemed to enjoy having Jim along for the escapade. The coyotes escaped unharmed. The dogs do keep life interesting.

It snowed and rained for half the day, turning the vegetation soft and wet and the clay soil into slippery mud. Although two federal livestock-protection-dog specialists were scheduled to meet with me in camp, the weather conditions won't allow it. They are officially snowed out, or I'm mudded in—either way, no one is coming in or going out of here for a while. The wet weather is supposed to last about three days,

Luv's Girl struggles to rid her feet of the mud balls
that accumulated after a freezing rain.

and I'm looking forward to it. I have everything I need for the animals and for me, so all is well. The moisture is fabulous after the long drought, and my girls haven't begun lambing yet.

I called Pete to report my muddy circumstances, since the specialists were going to meet with him as well. They were paying a visit to our range to learn the specifics about how we utilize guardians to defend our herds, but nature foiled their plans. Pete already knew my situation, and had informed the agents that the road accessing my remote location would be impassable. He also let me know that something had disturbed the animals at his ranch during the night, and that all the guardian dogs were on edge. His ranch has the nearest dwellings to my camp, about ten miles as the raven flies.

I took note of what he said, but didn't think much about it until later in the afternoon. All three guardian dogs were outside my camp, lying on the hillside, barking toward the badlands below. I went about what I was doing and the next I knew, the dogs were gone. I eventually saw them as they crossed over hilltops several miles away, in the direction of Pete's ranch. Within an hour or so, Rena returned, but the others did not. I could see them lingering on the distant hills. Evidently, some predator was worthy of continued attention. The sheep were in the opposite direction, under my supervision and with their constant companions, burros Bill and Hillary.

I was sitting in the truck later in the afternoon when Abe arrived at my door, crying to get in—something he's never done before. I opened the door and he jumped in, quivering in nervousness, sitting up every now and then to peer over the dashboard into the distant badlands. He was hearing something I couldn't, and the guardian dogs were once again gone from view.

Rant eventually appeared atop a rock pile in the badlands, while Luv's Girl remained elusive. Finally, Luv's Girl appeared outside the pasture on a hillside about half a mile distant. I hoped that the predator was no larger than a coyote, even though I know that a clever coyote can wreak a fair amount of destruction. My fear is that the ruckus at Pete's ranch, and here in the badlands, was caused by a wolf or wolves. It was 6 P.M. when a very muddy and tired Luv's Girl made it back to camp.

Livestock protection dogs have been raised for thousands of years to do one job—guard domestic livestock from predators. The dogs are extremely dedicated and brave, and it's these traits that often result in their deaths. Few people have ever witnessed a guardian dog encounter with a predator, let alone a large carnivore actually killing a guardian. Most of the time, a dog will simply disappear from its herd. Sometimes its carcass is found, but often it is not. Sometimes the dogs give their lives while successfully guarding their sheep, but sometimes the wolves prevail to the detriment of both sheep and dogs.

Researchers in Romania documented one pack of wolves that came to specialize in killing livestock protection dogs as a food source. In a two-year period in the early 2000s, this wolf pack was responsible for the deaths of 157 adult guardian dogs.

As I sit writing in my sheep camp, I think about my other shepherd friends and what they were experiencing with their sheep herds. One year my friend Mary had eleven ewes killed in one night on the mountain, with the wolves eating just a little on each one and mauling their guardian dog. The same year, another sheepman had a wolf pack come into his herd during the first week of August, killing thirteen lambs, two ewes, and two guardian dogs. I hear of these events and am chilled with the reminder that it could easily be me, and my herd. While this time it's two guard dogs belonging to someone else, it could just as easily be Rant and Rena, our beautiful, devoted guardians. We know that wolves killed eight of the livestock guardian dogs I raised that had gone on to other sheep producers. I make it a practice not to ask after the dogs anymore, because if they've come to such a fate, I don't want to know. It's too painful. Most livestock-protection-dog deaths to wolves happen when the dogs are outnumbered and outweighed by these predators. We need bigger dogs and more of them to have a chance at surviving conflicts with wolf packs.

Although wolves are a serious predator, they're really not so different from our guardian dogs when it comes to basic behaviors. Our guardian dogs pair-bond, just like wolves do. A female will pick her mate and the two begin to spend all their time together. They play, and run, and roughhouse, and romp. When they wrestle it's a beautiful dance, their legs intertwined and their bodies close as they rub their muzzles together. They become devoted to each other.

When the bitch (the wolf or the dog) is ready to have pups, she'll enter a secluded den. The male will run back and forth in nervous agitation, fussing over the female like any expectant father. Once the pups are born and begin to eat solid food, the female will leave the den to hunt, and then come back to regurgitate the food for her pups. I've watched our puppies run out of the natal den when the mother returns, jumping up to bite at her mouth to induce her to vomit. The den might be in a culvert or a ditch bank, part of a fallen tree, or under a building.

If you bother the pups in the den, the female will move them to a new den. Jim and Cass did that once, then had to follow the bitch to the new den to find out where she'd hidden her puppies.

Guardian dog puppies play-fight just like wolf pups. They will practice the stalk-and-stare method of attack. It's fun to watch, and by the time they are five-month-old muscular beasts, it can sure make the hair stand up on the back of your neck when you realize the power and prowess on display.

I never did learn what badlands predator had so disturbed our dogs that day.

In the last few decades, Europe has experienced an overall agricultural decline, with land abandonment and reforestation of formerly cultivated and grazed range. Government agencies and nongovernmental interests are now working to reverse this trend. Many European countries have adopted programs targeting agrotourism rather than ecotourism, focusing on the cultural landscape rather than a "wild" landscape to attract visitors. Some have expressed concerns that having countryside too wild would inhibit visitors, maintaining that rewilding the region while excluding human use results in an artificial state, detaching people from the culture and traditions of a region.

In addition, European governments are focused on how much of each nation's food supply is generated within its own borders, promoting national self-sufficiency and use of local resources.

While the United States does have some of these factors in common with our European counterparts, of more significance are current trends in public thinking such as the locavore movement to consume locally grown products; "slow food" promotions, shunning fast food; organic and natural-product niche food production and marketing expansion; and "green" agriculture, with its increasing public interest in the health effects of various types of food and food production.

Those who would rid the West of its livestock grazing and transhumance assert that public-land ranching is practiced by land barons who are brutal to their stock, continuing a lawless and violent tradition of early western cattlemen. Leaders of the antigrazing movement argue that there is a religious dimension to the "western myth" of ranching. Their warped logic goes something like this: biblical principles led to utilitarian attitudes toward the natural world, whereby believers claimed dominion over nature; these attitudes were embraced by those who settled and developed the West, leading to widespread overgrazing of the public range. Politicians and lobbyists aligned with the religious right seek to allow the devastation to continue. Following this line of reasoning, livestock grazing on public rangelands should be stopped.

Demonizing ranchers in this way makes it easier to see them as not fully human, thus not deserving of human rights. Some radical environmental activists advocate violence against ranchers and their livestock. Once you're to the point of using these tactics, there is no intelligent debate, just hatred.

Many of the ranchers I know have a fairly intimate relationship with their animals, knowing the animals' family lineages, histories, and behavioral tendencies. They tell stories about individual animals in their herds, and when processing their animals for handling, will often comment on their various personality quirks. I tell similar stories, because I know my sheep.

I feel a kinship with those around the world who live and work with their livestock, and I admire the close relationships other pastoralists have with their animals, relationships that are indeed sometimes based on religious beliefs. India's Muslim pastoralists with their water buffalo immediately come to mind, and the African Maasai with their cattle. These are beautiful people, with beautiful animals, living their lives with significant bonds to each other.

Livestock raised on the open range in the West include both domestic sheep and cattle. They aren't confined to feedlots, small pens, and barns, injected and fed precisely formulated and measured rations, their bodily wastes removed by humans. Range livestock move from pasture to pasture, migrating with the seasons, tended to by human herders or drovers. It's a natural cycle of food production, with the livestock eating the smorgasbord provided by nature, leaving waste behind to fertilize the ground.

Just as an illness will be transmitted from child to child in a schoolyard, the same happens to animals in confinement. Livestock scattered on open range tend to stay healthier, requiring less use of antibiotics or other medicines. Seasonal migrations make herds less susceptible to free-living parasites, and less at the mercy of nuisance biting insects. Strong animals survive and reproduce. Nature removes the weak animals from the food chain.

One inhabitant of this basin's arid rangelands is a small bird of prey called the western burrowing owl. An important component of burrowing-owl nesting is manure from livestock or bison. Although biologists originally believed the owls mainly used dried manure as nesting material, more recent research indicates that owls use insects associated with the manure as a major protein source during nesting.

Nesting underground in grasslands, shrub steppe, and disturbed areas like roadways, these little seven- to ten-inch-long birds have been called the "priests of prairie dogs," as they preside over burrows in prairie dog colonies, although nests are found in other areas as well.

Unlike most other owls, burrowing owls are most active during the day, with male owls often seen around the entrance to the burrow in daylight, venturing farther away at dawn and dusk. Research indicates that the males will collect a variety of vegetative matter around the entrance in order to lure insects within easy range. They will then provide the feed to mates and offspring inside the nesting burrow.

Owlets will begin leaving their natal den by about forty-five days. Burrowing owls also prey on meadow voles and small birds like horned larks. Badgers are the burrowing owl's primary predator.

Although much is known about the breeding and nesting habits of burrowing owls, little is known about their winter ecology. It's believed that the birds winter in Mexico and Central America. They arrive on our sheep range in April most years, and leave the Green River Basin before November.

Bulgaria is home to a number of vulnerable wildlife species listed as endangered by the International Union for Conservation of Nature, and several of these species are highly dependent on well-grazed open pastureland, with its high diversity of plant and insect life. Taking note of the restoration of transhumance in Spain and France, conservationists associated with the Fund for Wild Flora and Fauna, Bulgaria, are undertaking a program of their own. This nongovernmental organization owns a herd of 250 sheep of a rare native breed, the Karakachan. When local farmers experience sheep loss due to predation by protected carnivores, the group provides live sheep from its own herd as replacement animals. Its transhumance program features public education campaigns and a "shepherd school" for young people.

My involvement with nature is daily, and most often in association with my sheep herd and its guardian animals. Pastoralists throughout the world share similar experiences, becoming a part of the natural world in which they live.

India is a country rich in pastoralism: the Raikas, who tend to camels, the Van Gujjar nomads in the Himalayas, with their water buffalo, and the Ladakhs and their yaks, to name just a few. Yet all of these groups face similar problems with traditional grazing lands blocked due to creation of national parks, forest reserves, or sanctuaries. India's policy for national conservation areas restricts access to everyone but tourists. Although the Muslim Van Gujjar buffalo herders have migrated across northern India for at least fifteen hundred years, the creation of conservation areas resulted in pressure for nomads to become village residents and farmers, with thousands of Van Gujjars forced from traditional lands.

These pastoralists have been left out of conservation and land-management planning, and even Indian pastoralists who are working to provide for the continued existence of local breeds of livestock (cattle, sheep, and buffalo) fail to receive recognition or support for their work with rare breeds.

Tending to animals is a sacred duty in the cultural belief systems of certain Indian communities, and their livestock are important in the local economy. For example, certain cattle breeds such as the Pulikulam are used at night to fertilize fields, resulting in a 50 percent reduction in inorganic fertilizer costs for farmers using this service. At least one rare breed of sheep is used for the same purpose in India, and certain cattle breeds are commonly used as draft animals throughout the country. These various livestock breeds contribute to biodiversity, and are prized for their local adaptations, such as being disease-resistant, and their ability to thrive in harsh environments such as dry land zones.

Nevertheless, it has been estimated that every month one locally adapted livestock breed maintained with indigenous knowledge becomes extinct, replaced with more generic and "higher performance" breeds.

◇ ◇ ◇ ◇

Not only have livestock breeds disappeared, the people who tend these animals also find themselves threatened. The displacement or eviction of people from their traditional lands in the name of environmental conservation has become so widespread that a term has been coined to describe this group of people: conservation refugees. Organizations have been formed to support these displaced peoples, and books have been written to help tell their stories.

Conservation refugees exist on every continent except Antarctica. It has been said that conservation has exceeded resource extraction as the primary source of eviction of indigenous and traditional people from their lands. These people have been forced out by means of proscriptions against the use of historic lands and traditional practices.

Here in America, the situation is less dramatic than in other parts of the world. But the dynamics of displacing individuals involved with livestock are similar. Deals are quietly made behind closed doors, often in a federal agency office. A public-lands-grazing permittee, under pressure from all directions, is approached by a nongovernmental organization offering a hefty payday if the rancher will give up his animal unit months, his grazing pasture on public land. Once that deed is done, the US Forest Service, without any public involvement, but with full knowledge of the details of the private deal that just went down, agrees to not reissue the grazing permit to another permittee. More lands are closed to livestock grazing every year using this technique.

Some say that it's the permittee's decision to sell out. That's true, but this action of closing allotments without scrutiny certainly isn't sound public policy, and it doesn't help the livestock industry as a whole, or other livestock producers who would have welcomed the

A herd of pronghorn antelope race across the range.

opportunity to graze those allotments. There are also numerous ways
to turn a permittee into a "willing seller." Through deals like these, the
western livestock industry is putting itself out of business, one willing
seller at a time. The result is that vital links to the transhumance system are eliminated, no longer available for use. Other countries have
made the same mistakes, and are now trying to restore these grazing
systems, but for some reason, we fail to learn.

Some of the permit deals have been made with the justification of
reducing conflicts between livestock and endangered species. At first

blush, this might seem to make sense, but I doubt that biological re-covery of large carnivores like grizzly bears and gray wolves will stop the closures, since there seems to be no limit to the reasons proposed to close allotments to livestock grazing. When we partition off lands for favored interests, we soon find we've lost much land, along with our willingness to tolerate competing interests.

Allotments are also being closed and domestic sheep producers are being pushed from the mountains under the pretense of protect-ing a species that is not even endangered—Rocky Mountain bighorn sheep, a widely hunted trophy-game species. The closure of domestic-sheep allotments is being done to create buffers between wild sheep and domestic sheep—to reduce the *possibility* of risk of disease trans-mission from domestic sheep to bighorn sheep. Setting aside the sci-entific controversy over whether this assumed disease transfer actually occurs, rather than using techniques like active herding and guardian dogs to ensure separation of the species, allotment closure seems to be the preferred strategy. Agencies pushing for the allotment closures include the US Forest Service and state wildlife agencies, while groups like the Wild Sheep Foundation (formerly the Founda-tion for North American Wild Sheep) supply the money to buy out grazing allotments held by domestic-sheep producers.

Wild-sheep advocates contend that they support multiple use of public lands, and take deep offense to any comparison with groups advocating ending public-lands livestock grazing. The fact is that these same sheep advocates have joined antigrazing groups in litiga-tion aimed at getting certain sheep producers off mountain pastures. The tactics of the Wild Sheep Foundation have worked so well that those pushing to end livestock grazing on public lands are now using allotment buyouts as a method to achieve their goal as well. When you lie down with dogs, you wake up with fleas.

Wild-sheep managers note that there are less than fifty families in the western United States that graze domestic sheep on public lands in occupied bighorn sheep range, as if the loss of these families from the landscape would be minor. I personally know at least a dozen of these families, and the notion of their being removed from the range makes my heart ache. These same wild-sheep managers harp on what they call "hobby ranchers" who have sheep on private property anywhere near where bighorn sheep could possibly roam. I don't think these folks would stop at ridding the public lands of domestic sheep.

My great fear is that these same wild-sheep advocates, who now have an international focus rather than just North American interests, will begin the work of separating wild sheep from domestic sheep herded by my nomad friends in other high-elevation regions of the world. Beware my Mongolian friends, beware.

The storm started just before dark. After conducting the last sheep check of the day, Abe and I hurried into camp, hoping the herd would fare well. The wind blew wet snow from the east, pounding the side of the camp, pelting it with a covering of white slush. From my window I watched the sheep on the skyline above me until they disappeared in the squall. Thunder accompanied the snow, making the storm even more disconcerting. I awoke during the night as the wind gusts increased and worried about the herd. Heavy wet snow—this is sheep-killing weather.

Arising before dawn, I drove to the top of the hill behind the camp and was heartened to see a barely discernable dark form in the tall sagebrush on the neighboring hillside. It was the two burros standing together, and as I studied the landscape around them, I noticed that the hillside was a slightly different shade than the surrounds—the sheep were there, filling in the gaps among the brush. It was a good place to huddle, protected in the brush from the nearly six inches of new snow. I later discovered two ewes in a draw near my camp, separated from the herd, with Rant hiding in the brush above them. This could mean lambing was about to begin.

I finally spotted Luv's Girl when she stood up in the sagebrush to get my attention. She was on another hillside near my camp, guarding a dead ewe. I patted her neck as I inspected her still-warm body—she hadn't gone into labor yet, and there was no sign of predator damage. The cold, wet wind was too much for the older ewe, and she never arose from her bed. The death of a ewe always makes me sad, but I do

---

Overleaf: Luv's Girl oversees the birth from her hiding place
in the thick brush, staying close but not bothering.

know that death is part of life. Living on a ranch, I am often reminded of that.

I couldn't leave such a predator attractant near my camp, so I tied the ewe's front legs to the hitch of my pickup truck with a rope, and dragged the two-hundred-pound body, sliding through the mud and slush, into a draw about a mile away, on the next allotment over, where there were no livestock. I took her as far as I thought I could, considering the sloggy hill I would have to traverse in four-wheel drive to get back to my camp and the rest of the herd. When I cut the rope off her legs, I positioned the body as if it were at rest. I hoped that she had simply gone to sleep in the brush and never woken up—a gentle death, unlike the death that would be inflicted on her herd members had I left her carcass nearby to draw in coyotes, ravens, and any other neighborhood predators.

I couldn't get any news on the truck radio, but Jim called to say there was a winter storm warning in effect until midnight. Of course all this wet slush meant that I was snowed in again, with no way to get out or for others to get in. I'm prepared for this: my camp is well equipped with supplies for both the animals and myself. I have a small medical kit, and a large veterinary kit. And being isolated on the range makes me more mindful of my activities and not to take unnecessary risks.

Of course, this life is full of risks; it is part of being in nature, and I would not have it any other way. It saddens me that in today's society, children are increasingly kept indoors to protect them from potential dangers, and when allowed to venture out to explore nature, they are often in structured areas like parks with numerous restrictions (Don't Walk on the Grass; Stay on the Trails), and told to Look, but Don't Touch.

Richard Louv, in his 2005 book *Last Child in the Woods*, argues that children are developing "nature deficit disorder," resulting in a number of behavioral problems. Besides the negative health effects of a sedentary indoor existence, attention disorders and depression are a growing problem in youth that the solace of the outdoors may help alleviate.

Louv explains that humans have an instinctive yearning for nature, and under the "biophilia hypothesis," humans are still basically hunter-gatherers and need "at some level we don't fully understand, direct involvement with nature." If we don't get that, we don't do so well. So goes the theory.

When I went back to check the herd after dealing with the dead ewe, I encountered our first lamb of the season, staggering around on strong legs next to its mother. The lamb was yellow-colored from the amniotic fluid of the birth sac, but seemed healthy. Rena found the lamb not long after I did, and lay down in the brush below the ewe and her babe, guarding unobtrusively. After a while, I spotted a nervous young ewe with a dirty nose, a sign that she had recently cleaned off a newborn lamb. As the herd moved off and the wind began gusting once again, this young ewe spooked and ran along with it, looking back into the brush a couple of times on her way. I went down the hill and over to the brush, and found a cold lamb, alive but not standing. I tried to herd the mother back to the lamb, but no such luck. Soaking wet after running around in the slush, I picked up the lamb and carried it up the hill to the truck.

Back at camp, I prepared some lamb-milk replacer for the lamb and heated a bottle. Wrapping the dirty, chilled baby in my sweatshirt, I placed it across my lap, using my left thumb to pry open its cold mouth far enough so that I could get the soft latex nipple into its mouth with the other hand. The lamb was still, unmoving. I took off one of my warm wool socks and used it to rub the babe's face and throat, prompting the swallowing reflex. A few drops of warm milk finally entered her cold body. Using my hands, I rubbed her ribs and hips vigorously, as a mother ewe does with her tongue, to stimulate blood flow. The lamb's legs felt cold to the touch, and she arched her neck back in a movement we call the death stretch, because this is what lambs typically do as they die. I cuddled her to my chest, forcing a few more warm drops down her throat, using my head and neck to gently place her head back toward her front feet, in a position of life.

Knowing I was wearing out an already completely exhausted animal, I wrapped the lamb in my coat and placed her in a chair in front of the heater. Every five minutes or so I rotated the chair, alternating her body's exposure to the heat, and eventually her legs and body were warm to the touch. Every ten minutes, I squeezed a few more drops of warm milk into her mouth. She soon began to raise her head on her own, opening her eyes and looking at me as I fed her, shivering in response to the changes in her body temperature. Within the hour, she made her first soft tugs on the nipple, the sucking impulse necessary for survival finally coming back to her. It gave me hope. I know that if I can get half an ounce of warm milk into a cold lamb during the first few hours of its life, I stand a chance of saving it.

I made a pot of hot tea, leaving the bottle floating in the pot, keeping the milk warm for those frequent feedings. By lunchtime, the tiny lamb's head was up, eyes bright and alert, nose poking around in her bedding, and she began softly bleating her complaint that she was hungry. She drank an ounce in one feeding, and I knew that she had made it through the worst. Soon she began kicking off her covers, struggling to stand. Feedings continued every hour or so, one or two ounces at a time. She was a big girl, and wanted plenty of nourishment. Rena insisted on coming into the camp to watch over the new baby. I hoped the other ewe and lamb were warm enough tucked into the sagebrush, but knowing my disturbance could be fatal if I caused the lamb to stand and lose body heat, I left them alone.

Outside, the wind continued to howl, with snow sputtering from the sky. If only we can survive this day, tomorrow's sunshine will breathe new life across this landscape.

Just a few fencelines over from this lambing ground, Doc Jensen raises beef cattle on his ranch in the foothills of the Wind River Mountains. When winter sets in and the snow gets deep, elk move to lower country, grazing near his cattle herd. Years ago, the Wyoming Game and Fish Department established an elk feedground nearby to keep the elk, in danger of starving, away from cattle feed-lines.

But in 2003 something went wrong. Several cattle belonging to Doc's herd tested positive for brucellosis, a highly contagious disease of hooved animals that can cause animals to abort their calves. His ranch was placed under quarantine, prohibiting the movement of animals on or off the ranch. All of Doc's herd had to be gathered into corrals and blood samples drawn. About one-third of the animals tested seropositive for the disease, and the final result was that Doc's entire herd—nearly four hundred animals—had to be slaughtered. It was heartbreaking for Doc and his family.

The story didn't end there. All neighboring cattle herds, and any herds that had fenceline contact with these herds, were quarantined and tested. The testing program was extended outward to thousands of cattle. Meanwhile it was determined that the brucellosis contracted by Doc Jensen's cattle herd was the same disease type carried by the nearby elk, confirming that transmission from wildlife to livestock had occurred.

The intensive testing program in Wyoming eventually resulted in several more cattle herds being sent to slaughter. These herds had intermingled with wild elk and/or bison in the Yellowstone region. As

Elk on a nearby feedground were responsible for spreading disease to local cattle herds.

long as infected wildlife remains in the region, transmission of disease to cattle is an ongoing threat. Another infected cattle herd was discovered in western Wyoming in 2008. The entire herd of six hundred cattle, which grazed an area inhabited by elk, was sent to slaughter.

Part of Wyoming's livestock and wildlife disease-prevention program emphasizes keeping cattle and elk separated during the period of the year considered high risk for disease transmission. Cattle ranchers in western Wyoming feed cattle on their private land in the winter months, and much effort is made to keep elk and cattle from commingling during that time. Although some commingling occurs on many ranches in the region, it is just for limited time periods until the animals can be separated. There is much work being done to combat this disease, from vaccinating both elk and cattle, to a pilot test-and-slaughter program to remove infected elk from the population. Even the vaccine used by cattle ranchers is not 100 percent effective at keeping their herds safe.

Some wildlife advocates are pushing for the closure of the elk feedgrounds, since the concentration of animals during the high-risk period sets the stage for disease transmission. It's an option, but the outcome could be devastating. If the feedgrounds were closed, large-scale elk die-offs due to starvation would be expected, with a decrease in western Wyoming's elk population of 70 to 80 percent. The feedgrounds help to keep elk away from private property, which helps to prevent damage to stored feed such as hay on ranches, and feeding elk prevents cattle and elk from coming into contact, reducing disease-transmission risks from wildlife to livestock. No system is perfect though, as the loss of Doc's herd proved.

Federal and state wildlife and animal health officials have a goal to eliminate brucellosis from the Yellowstone region's bison and elk populations. The national brucellosis-eradication program has cost over $3.5 billion. With a 50 percent brucellosis seroprevalence rate in bison, and a 35 percent seroprevalence rate in elk, the task before them is daunting. Wyoming's effort to keep wintering elk and cattle separated seems like a rational step in combating disease.

By late afternoon the orphan lamb had taken over the camp, climbing out of the hay-filled feed tub I'm using as her bed, peeing on the floor, and curling up in front of the heater, her favorite place. She's very vocal, calling to me often, and soon she's practicing her bucks and running the length of the camp floor. I leave her locked inside the camp, sometimes with Rena but other times alone, while I check the herd.

Rena watches over the orphan lamb inside my camp.

Just prior to sunset, and for the first time all day, a few patches of blue sky become visible over the Wind River Mountains. It brings me hope for fair weather in the morning, although the wind is blowing as night falls once again.

The lamb "talked" through much of the night, softly bleating in an attempt to get me to respond and reveal my whereabouts in the dark, and to convince me to get up and feed her. Her persistent and at times demanding calls drew the attention of the guardian dogs, who surrounded the camp whining, crying, and barking, pleading with me in frustration to let them have the baby or to do *something*.

Responding as I would to any baby crying out during the night, I spoke to her softly, getting a gentle murmur in return, but other times she bleated loudly, with an emphasis at the end of her outburst as though she were asking a question: "Now, Mama?"

"No dear, go back to sleep."

I gave up at 2 A.M. and fed her a few ounces of milk, but she continued her demands until I got up for good three hours later. I fumbled in the dark to start the coffee pot and pot of hot water for the lamb's bottle, then sat and waited for them to heat. When I turned on a flashlight I discovered that my camp had been newly decorated with random wet spots accompanied by a splattering of yellow lamb poop here and there. For those without such knowledge, poop from a newborn lamb is its own shade of bright yellow—so distinct I've always thought it should be a crayon color.

I dressed and slipped my feet into my slippers, only to discover the left one was damp inside. I slid my foot back out, and shone the light at the slipper. Yep, she had peed in it too.

It was nearly thirty degrees when I stepped outside for the first check of the herd—beautiful weather. As I approached the sheep, I could see one ewe off in a draw by herself, so I figured she had just given birth. Yesterday's newborn lamb was up and hollering at its mother, inspecting other sheep in the herd, and generally causing a ruckus. Luv's Girl and the burros stood by as calm overseers.

All being well with the herd, I turned my attention back to the ewe off by herself, but by that time she was no longer alone. I could see her lamb standing up underneath her as three ravens harassed her, trying to get her to flee. I hurried Rena down to the scene, moving the ewe and lamb away from the birthing location and shooing the ravens off. Rena began cleaning up the birth matter, which I hoped would discourage the ravens' return.

But the birds had simply gone off to bother the larger herd, the nasty buggers. I scared them off once again, but I know that if there isn't some control put on these black beasts of the air soon, some of my herd will meet a tragic end.

I went back to camp to feed the orphan lamb, which I had situated in a cozy two-horse stock trailer with a pile of alfalfa hay. Rant was guarding the entrance to the trailer when I arrived, and when I went inside with the bottle, he leaned through the door to clean the lamb's butt, then cleaned the milk from her face once her meal was complete. Good guardian. Ewes will keep their lamb's butt clean by licking, but in the absence of the ewe, it seems our guardian dogs take over this parental behavior with orphan lambs. I went off to check the herd again, leaving Rant to protect the camp's new occupant.

The yellow lamb that had been born in the storm was not doing well. It had been alive for twenty-four hours, so I knew it had to have eaten at some point, but it was crying on the lambing ground. When the herd moved off to graze, the mother attempted to follow, but the lamb curled up in a draw and refused to go any farther. I checked the sleeping lamb and discovered its belly was empty—that's why it had been crying. The ewe returned to her lamb and I could see her bag was full of milk, but her teats had swollen to such a size, the lamb, with its tiny mouth, could not grab hold. Eventually the ewe left the lamb and returned to the herd. I kept my eye on the babe, concerned about the ravens, and returned to camp just long enough to grab a milk bottle. When I picked up the lamb, which was not yellow anymore because of the rain and snow, its mouth was cold. As soon as I stuck the nipple in its mouth, the lamb drank strongly, quickly draining the three ounces available in the bottle. I waited around about ten minutes, but its mother didn't return, so I made the decision to take it back to camp.

Once there, I left the lamb on the seat of the truck with the heater blazing while I heated another bottle. I hoped the company of my other orphan would do this one some good. Two lambs are actually easier to take care of than one. Lambs will stimulate each other, including with respect to food competition. They also cuddle up together, sharing body heat and companionship, important for such social creatures.

I fed both lambs and locked them in the stock trailer, but not before Rant inspected them, cleaned their butts, and later lay his massive body down to guard the door that sheltered his tiny charges.

This was not exactly a stellar start to lambing, but a live lamb is better than a dead lamb. There is also a chance I may be able to get these lambs back in the care of a mother ewe, but the ewe with the full bag needs to be caught first. I know better than to try to catch a two-hundred-pound hormonal ewe when I'm out here in camp by myself. If I get hurt, I'm no help to anyone or anything. Weather permitting, Jim and Cass will try to drive in this evening and catch her for me. Time will tell, since once again a major winter storm is hitting the state, with road closures nearly everywhere but here in this upper portion of the basin.

The next time I went to check the sheep, they were climbing up the back side of Coyote Rocks. I climbed the rocks from the front side and met some ewes along the top. One ewe was beginning labor

I wrapped the lamb in my coat, and left it
on the seat of the truck to warm up.

while she grazed, but she was apparently trying hard to ignore it, although she turned her head every few minutes to look toward her rear end. I could see her labor pains intensify and two little hooves sticking out her backside, but she refused to lie down and push. Instead, she continued to walk and graze, then would stop and squat, pushing all the while. Eventually she lay down and was up again very quickly, spinning around to face the scary moving mess of lamb she'd just deposited on the ground. She stepped back, looked at the mess, then charged forward as if to butt it, but began vigorously licking it instead. She repeated this action several times in her nervousness, this first-time mother. I left the new pair alone, figuring the ewe had the situation under control. I returned just over an hour later to find that the ewe's troubles had doubled. She now had two lambs, and was busy tending to both.

I returned to camp for a hot bowl of tomato soup and a cold glass of wine, watching out the window as a storm crept slowly down the west face of the Wind Rivers, headed in my direction. By the time it arrived later in the afternoon it was just a sputtering of snow, and I was thankful for that, because several more ewes chose that same time to begin lambing. By the time the day was over, two sets of twins and three singles had been born. Jim and Cass did make it to camp, bringing pizza from town, and helped me catch and load the ewe with the swollen bag and teats into the trailer, to reunite her with the lamb I'd taken earlier in the day. The ewe had a bad injury to her front shoulder, a deep stab wound as if she had run into something sharp, and she had blood in her milk as well. Jim and Cass drained her udder and fed the two lambs while I checked on the herd's other new babes. We left the injured ewe with both lambs in the trailer, in hopes that maybe she'd at least take her own back, if not adopt the other lamb as well.

Not long after my family departed, I fell into my sleeping bag early, exhausted.

The next day's predawn check renewed my hopes for lambing season. I took a hot cup of coffee with me on my early-morning round, running the truck's heater to ward off the chill of a thick layer of frost as I inspected the new lambs scattered across the pasture. I found the sheep still bedded in a stand of sagebrush, the two burros and a guardian dog in their midst, and soon glimpsed Rant as he stood up from his post on the neighboring hilltop. Assured that the herd was well cared for, I headed for the twins that were born yesterday on the eastern side of Coyote Rocks, and found the ewe and her two babes at ease. With two more ewes and their lambs to check out to the west, I headed in that direction, only to notice movement in the rocks above me. Both of the ewes had moved their lambs up into the protection of the rocks—good mothers. Counting my blessings, I drove back to camp, encountering Rena on the way, and giving her a ride to breakfast.

The ewe left in the trailer with her own lamb and the orphan was very concerned about both, showing she has good maternal instincts, but the blood in her milk was a concern. I supplemental-fed both lambs as I debated what to do. Closer observation of the ewe's lamb revealed that it was suffering from a sore back leg; maybe that's why the babe hadn't been able to keep up with the herd.

Orphan lambs are called bums because they'll try to survive by stealing milk from various ewes in the herd. Mother ewes, especially those with twins, quickly become used to their lambs attacking their milk bags numerous times throughout the day; it's such a frequent occurrence, some ewes continue grazing without even lifting their heads. It's these unsuspecting ewes that bums prey on, and you can tell a bum in a herd by its dirty head, since it often sneaks up on the milk bag from behind.

Confident that the herd's lambs were in good hands, I drove around the pasture to check on the available forage. In the northern section, I was amazed at the amount of sage grouse scat I found. There were small piles of it every foot or so, covering the ground in one area. On one of his visits Jim had explored this section of the northern fenceline and reported hearing the repeated low rumble of drums. He had been listening to activity on a sage grouse lek. Leks are traditional communal breeding grounds used by North America's largest grouse, the greater sage grouse, which can weigh up to seven pounds.

Every morning around sunrise in March and April, sage grouse can be found on leks throughout the basin. Male grouse are in their prime for breeding season, ready to perform elaborate strutting displays to impress the hens. Grouse use a variety of locations for leks, but prefer open areas, usually surrounded by sagebrush, their primary food source. Sage grouse in the West have been on the decline in recent years—environmentalists have petitioned that they be listed as endangered—but this basin still hosts one of the largest grouse populations on earth.

Male grouse have a large white ruff around their necks and bright

yellow air sacks on their breasts and are much larger than the females, which are a mottled brown, black, and white color. The males
also have long filoplumes arising off the backs of their necks, and yellow eye combs. Two yellow air sacks located on their upper breasts
are inflated during mating displays, making a deep popping sound
somewhat like a drumbeat, which can be heard for long distances.

During intense encounters on leks, male sage grouse stand side-
by-side or face-to-face and often erupt in wing fights as they try to
force the other to retreat. They snap their beaks and slap each other

A male sage grouse struts his stuff on a traditional breeding ground.

with their wings. Soon after sunrise, the birds disappear, some flying into the distance, others seeking cover in the surrounding sage.

One cold morning as I was leaving a grouse lek, I noticed there were more grouse out in the thermal cover provided by thick stands of sagebrush than were actually using the lek that day. Two male grouse were next to the road; one wandered away into the brush as I approached, but the other remained.

I was driving our noisy flatbed GMC ranch feed truck, which emits a low rumble while it idles (teenagers love it), so I turned off the motor to quietly observe the bird. After a minute or two the bird turned to enter the brush. Thinking the show was over, I fired up the truck to go. The noise attracted the bird, which then spun around to challenge the GMC. He strutted and puffed out the air sacks on his chest numerous times, making a drumming noise, tail feathers fanned out behind him. When I shut the truck off again, he calmed back down and started to walk away, but whirled and resumed his prancing when I revved the engine. Apparently the noise of the truck was at the correct decibel level to be of interest to the bird—at least this individual bird.

I was so entertained by his antics, I watched the male sage grouse for an hour or so before leaving. The bird remained, obviously winning the battle against the GMC for breeding rights to the territory.

Driving back to camp, I decided to check on Luv's Girl, who hadn't come off the bedding ground when the sheep moved off to begin grazing. I found her overseeing the birth of a new pair of lambs. Curled up in the underbrush at an acceptable distance, the dog seemed to be a welcome presence for the ewe.

Wyoming's domestic sheep once numbered in the millions, but remain at less than half a million now. Most sheep in the western half of the state are those involved in seasonal migrations, since most of the western portion is public land. The eastern side of the state is predominately private land, with sedentary herds. Many of today's sheep producers in Wyoming are descendants of immigrants from the old country who came here to herd on the open range, usually for someone else. They took their wages in the form of sheep, and eventually bought private ground from which to base their own enterprises. Many came from the Basque country of France and Italy.

Italy's famed Abruzzo mountainous region, long known for its culture of transhumance, is now subject to concerted efforts to restore this type of pastoralism for which it is so famous. Like occurrences in other European countries, villages declined with the movement of people to more urban areas in recent years, and those remaining out in the countryside are aging. The Abruzzo's domestic sheep population dropped from 1.5 million to 400,000 over the last one hundred years, with mosaic-patterned pasturelands deteriorating into scrubland and lacking diversity. Labor-intensive management practices, including sheep tending, have fallen out of favor, and modernization of irrigation has led to intensification of agriculture in some areas. It is hoped that Europe's newfound interest in traditional agriculture will help to revive the region.

One transhumance route in central Italy, the Royal Shepherd's Track, has been nominated for consideration as a World Heritage Site because of its combined historic and environmental value. This trail is nearly two hundred miles in length, and believed to have been used for a thousand years.

❖ ❖ ❖ ❖

A light snow had been falling all morning, and in my drive around the pasture I was stunned at the resiliency of the plant life in this high-elevation, cool-season environment. As the snow melts, it reveals collections of tiny blooming flowers resembling downy pincushions scattered across the ground. For these minuscule gems to not only survive but flourish in such harsh climatic conditions is remarkable. The cushion phlox is one of the most common flowers in the sagebrush steppe, and its blooms blanket windswept slopes with early-season color.

Jim refers to the cushion plant community as "the evolution of small," since many cushion plants are miniature, specialized versions of larger, more widespread species. These drought-resistant plants have evolved to survive the region's long winters, strong winds, and cold temperatures, as well as close grazing by herbivores and erosion events caused by the fragile soils they are often associated with. Their shape allows them to hold moisture and reduce evaporation, and some of these small mounds have thick, woody roots that reach far into the earth for water.

Found amid the cushion plant community is the short-horned lizard, commonly known as the horned toad, which kids will hunt for like lost treasure. These small ant-eating reptiles give birth to live young, which can yield an easy feast for predators ranging from the shrike to the coyote. But the horned toad has an effective defense mechanism—its ability to disappear into its environment. Horned toads match the color of the habitat in which they are found and tend to remain motionless when in danger. But should a predator find, catch, and eat a horned toad, the reptile's body armor ensures it won't be a pleasant experience.

My troublesome predator once again is the raven. The afternoon check revealed three ewes with their five lambs comfortable atop Coyote Rocks. To the south of my camp I saw three ravens alight in the brush, but with the snowfall limiting my vision I couldn't be sure what the focus of their attention was. I loaded Rena in the truck and drove in for a closer look. We flushed the ravens from their perches around a young ewe and her first lamb. The ewe, comfortable in our presence, continued to talk to and clean off her babe, and Rena and I kept our distance to give the pair some privacy. I left Rena there to attend to matters, and headed back to camp.

As the snow continued to fall in the afternoon, I once again headed to Coyote Rocks to check the nursery bunch that had converged there. The russet-colored kestrel escorted me down the fenceline, flitting from post to post in front of me as I traveled along in the truck. As I turned toward Coyote Rocks, I noticed what appeared to be a large avian near the top of a rock. I suspected it was a raven, but when I trained my binoculars on the form I discovered it was a golden eagle. As I approached, the eagle took to the air. I continued around the back side of the rocks, where I found my mothers and babes, none the worse for the weather or our predatory neighbors.

the buck that stopped here

◇ ◇ ◇

Each check of the sheep herd reveals new lambs being born every few hours. It's late May and we're now in the heart of lambing season. The herd is becoming more scattered as ewes drop away here and there for privacy. The dogs and burros are busy, trying to keep up. Although the weather is being more kind, the sheep are most vulnerable to predation as they disperse to give birth.

Jim arrived to spend the night and help me move camp. We relocate it every week or two to stay close to the herd as it moves from pasture to pasture, and also to reduce the amount of trampling on vegetation and damage incurred from my presence. As we pulled up stakes, I decided to turn the ewe we'd been keeping in the trailer back out with the herd, concerned that she isn't producing enough milk for the bums and knowing that her lamb, with its bad leg, isn't going to survive. Sometimes, despite my best efforts, a lamb simply shows little interest in living. This lamb seemed dull, as if life was gradually departing from its body. The ewe's shoulder injury had healed, so she'll be fine on the range. The first of the bums is still very vocal and attentive, so I set her free outside the camp while Jim and I worked. She was excited but also nervous, staying right underfoot the entire time. I'd taken to calling her Paula, after Paula Simmons, who'd written an excellent book on sheep care, and, since the lamb was so darned vocal, Paula Poundstone, a favorite standup comedian.

The new campsite is only two ridges over from my former windswept locale, but at a lower elevation, beside the tall sagebrush. The birdsong bursting forth from the brush, startling in its volume and beauty, informed me that I had moved into sage thrasher habitat.

Overleaf: Our pronghorn buck is a part of the scenery now.

Several birds of this species sat atop the brush and regaled me noisily, laying claim to their territory.

After Jim departed for home, I went into the camp, where Paula could hear me but not see me. She fussed and cried, running forlornly back and forth outside until she finally gave up, curled up next to Rant's snoring mass, and fell asleep.

Rena accompanied me on the next lap of the pasture, checking on all the new lambs and mothers. I gave any ewes in labor about two hours to get the job done without my intervention, taking mental notes of where they were in the birthing process so I would know which ones needed revisiting on the next check. Rena and I walked near the reservoir, with Rena sniffing around in the brush as I explored all the multicolored rocks blanketing the earth. As we walked, with Rena following along behind me at a distance, I noticed a pronghorn antelope that had its eye on the dog and was rushing in for a closer look.

Oh no, not him again, I thought. In the last few days, this young, bold buck had been behaving badly enough that I had considering sending the herding dog out to teach him a lesson. The buck had made its presence known soon after our arrival, when I watched him saunter down the hill approaching the herd slowly for a closer look. When he'd sufficiently sized the sheep up he raced into the middle of the herd, scattering it and making the ewes run. I thought the buck was being territorial, and figured that was the end of it.

In the following days, the buck returned on numerous occasions, grazing alongside the ewes and not showing any further signs of aggression. That is, with the exception of the day I was trying to shepherd the sheep up over a hill to intercept a smaller group that had become separated. The buck had his eye on Abe and me as we worked, and came in closer and closer. I was curious how far in he would venture, so I let him approach within about thirty yards before I hollered and waved my arms to spook him. He ran off a little ways, but quickly turned to regain ground, though remaining at the edge of the herd.

Now I watched the buck as he keyed on Rena. The black glands on the sides of his neck were swollen, and the shock of hair on the back of his neck was erect, as was his white butt patch. Although both males and females have horns, pronghorn bucks can be identified by their black cheek patches. The cheek patches cover scent glands and vary in size with the season, swelling to about twice their normal size during the fall rut or breeding season. This buck was swollen out of season; he was a mess of hormones.

Rena is not allowed to chase pronghorn, and usually doesn't give them a bother, but this time she was irked by the buck's interest. She hurriedly walked to me, with the buck trotting along closely behind her. She flopped down at my feet, and that was enough to give the buck pause. Instead of coming closer, he pretended to graze on sagebrush nearby, as he used his front hooves to dig a little in the dirt, and then urinated in the scrape, marking his territory. I marveled at his antics as Rena and I got into the truck and drove away, leaving the temperamental beast on his own.

In the evening, Rant and I took Paula for a walk. She ran back and forth between us, enthusiastic and energetic. She would race forward in a short burst of speed, come to an abrupt halt to look around, and then sprint forward again. When we got to the end of the ridge, Rant spotted a few ravens harassing sheep in the valley below and set off to give chase. I turned the other way, toward the spring, but Paula fol-

A pronghorn antelope buck took a particular interest
in my herd—and in Rena.

lowed Rant. Once he realized the lamb was on his tail, Rant inter-
rupted his mission. He turned his heavy head to look back at his tiny
companion, then veered straight for me, the lamb in tow. Brushing up
against my leg, he left his follower at my side before turning to continue on with his work. I laughed as he fell into his rocking lope, in a
hurry to get away.

It was a warm, frost-free night. The coyotes were noisy in their aggression, making sure the dogs never rested. Since they are feeding pups in their dens by now, I expect an increase in trouble.

I was out in the truck before sunrise for the first sheep check, and headed to the west of camp first after spotting the dim outline of a large dog lying on a hill. As I approached, Rant stood and wagged his entire butt in enthusiasm. He wanted to show me something. I got to the top of his hill to find ten ewes and their newborn lambs scattered in the swale below. Rant could not have been more proud than if he had sired the lambs himself. I rubbed his ear stubs and scratched the base of his tail as I told him what a "good babboo" he was, and he leaned against me and wiggled his butt even more. I left the big lug and drove to the south to check on the burros, which I could see in the distance. They were between Rant's nursery herd and the southern fenceline, apart from the sheep. I figured their location was strategic, since most of the coyote noise had come from the south during the night. The burros would be the first obstacles a predator would encounter in an attempt to gain access to the sheep.

Rena was to the northwest of my camp, with a ewe and the twin lambs she was just starting to clean off. There were about four other ewes and lambs on a neighboring hillside just below, so these girls were using the proximity to camp in their favor.

The main herd was located on the highest hill in the pasture, with Luv's Girl's bright-white curled-up body visible even in the faint light. She was sleeping among the herd, providing a steady and calm measure of protection.

The burros came into camp shortly after breakfast, receiving their formal introduction to Paula. They followed her around outside the camp, gently breathing in her scent, careful with their movements in the presence of the baby.

A federal animal-damage-control agent named Rod visited the camp later in the day, there to respond to my pleas for raven relief. My injured bum lamb had finally died during the night, and Rod took the carcass and used it to bait the ravens into a favorite perch, where poison-laced morsels greeted them. Ironic that in order to halt the threat of ravens killing my lambs, we are feeding one of my lambs to those same ravens. The agent monitored the perch from a distance to be sure no raptors became unintended targets, and while he was thus engaged I noticed a group of ravens harassing the ewe and her twin lambs below my camp. Abe and I went off to intervene, finding a ewe so frazzled from warding off the birds, she'd decided to focus her efforts on protecting her largest lamb, abandoning the smaller one to seek cover in the brush. We'd arrived just in time. I grabbed the tiny babe and folded her into the front of my shirt to take to camp. Her umbilical cord was still damp, and although she was strong, her belly was empty.

The new lamb is less than half the size of our week-old Paula. Her diminutive form gave rise to the name Dimmy. I feed Dimmy three times more frequently than Paula, because she can take in only tiny amounts each time. Paula is put out that the arrival of a companion for her once again reduces her to captivity rather than freedom to roam around the camp with the dogs.

As I step out of the camp and walk through the sage, mourning doves coo soothingly and the sweet smell of the blooming phlox wafts up from the flowered hillsides and draws below, reminiscent of the rich honeysuckle aroma of my youth.

It's another warm, beautiful morning, with temperatures nearing forty degrees and a slight breeze holding out the promise of a possible rain shower drifting through the basin. It was a loud and rough night for the guardian animals—the coyotes were noisy, nearby, and aggressive, but most of the herd bedded on the same ridge as my camp, and the other small bunch, complete with their burros, were two hills over, within sight of camp.

I had arisen at 4:30 A.M., wakened by the sound of Dimmy's hungry cries coming from the livestock trailer. I heated a bottle and fed the bums by the light of a flashlight, then returned to camp to fill my coffee cup. Driving out for the first morning check, I found Rant fussing about something down in a sage-covered draw. It was a several-hours-old lamb, and since no ewes were claiming it, I grabbed the babe and put it in the truck. I continued on my rounds and was headed back to camp when I saw one ewe still on the bedding ground, upside down on her back in a draw, with the front half of a lamb sticking out her backside. She was obviously in distress, so I hurried over to help her get upright. She rewarded me by jumping to her feet, at which time the lamb fell to the ground in a splash and the ewe turned and ran over the ridge, never stopping to look back. I did the same, but in the opposite direction, hoping that the ewe would follow me and thereby return to her newborn lamb. No such luck. The abandoned lamb was huge, and the ewe had apparently labored strenuously. I left the lamb in the care of Rant for cleaning while I went back to camp to feed the new bums.

Afterward I located the ewe I believed to be the abandoned lamb's mother, but in the meantime she had given birth to another babe and was satisfied with having just one; it didn't seem worth the effort to try to force her other lamb back on her. I went to retrieve her firstborn from Rant, and found him with the lamb encircled in his front legs, gently licking and sniffing the young thing whose entire body was the size of his massive head. I praised him and picked up the lamb, which Rant was not pleased about; he jumped up possessively, nervously chomping his jowls and clicking his huge teeth together. Jim pointed out to me later that anyone else trying to take the lamb away from Rant probably would have lost an arm, and I knew as soon as he said it that this was true. Rant is uncompromisingly fierce in his devotion to the newborns, but fortunately he defers to me as he does to no other human. A gentle thump of my index finger on his head brings him to the ground in a quivering mess of apology. Rant trusts that I won't do anything bad to his baby lambs. Both of the two new bums are very large, and I wonder which one of our bucks is throwing these big beasts. It's a wonder the ewes are able to give birth without assistance.

We are a full week into lambing now, and my guess is that the herd is about one-quarter of the way done. With the exception of the one on her back this morning, none of the ewes has needed assistance in the birthing process, and the lambs are doing well. There are a few problems—I see a lamb limping on a front leg, and another that may not be getting enough milk. If they grow weak enough that I am able

Overleaf: The burros are a reassuring presence on the lambing ground.

to catch them, I will add these to my bum bunch. I have made attempts to run them down and knock them off their feet, and I have the bruises to prove it. But for the most part, the lambs sleep and play at their mothers' sides, moving with the herd, and all is well.

I have more bum lambs than I would like, but I keep reminding myself that a live lamb is better than a dead lamb. Of course, the best lamb is the one that is at its mother's side. Not only is it a lot of work to care for orphans, but the lamb-milk replacer I mix to feed them a half-dozen times a day is expensive. Raising orphan lambs is a risky proposition, since they may or may not survive, and the expense of feeding them could be more than the lamb is worth financially. I know all that, but I also know I love the way young lambs look into my eyes when I get that warm milk into their bodies, and the sense of accomplishment I feel knowing that I've been able to save a lamb from a cold death. It's worth it in the end, when I raise a ewe lamb from a bottle, only to have her friendly face in the herd, showing me her newborn lambs a few years later.

Young ewes having their first lambs are sometimes confused about what is happening to their bodies. I had one young ewe that was hysterical yesterday because she was about to have a lamb and didn't know what was happening. She kept trying to turn and look at her butt, but of course all she was doing was walking in circles. She was much calmer today, since she had finally given birth to a lamb and fallen madly in love with it.

One spring we had a high percentage of our ewes give birth to triplets. But that year our ewes weren't the only critters having triplets —it was just as common to see our local pronghorn does busy with triplet fawns as well. The mechanisms of natural systems are fascinating, and we often notice that our domestic sheep and local prong-horn antelope herds have some of the same behaviors and habits. The division between wild and domestic is not so great after all.

Jim called with good news this morning. My fourteen-year-old ewe, Friendly, gave birth to a large, bright white ewe lamb at home. Friendly was a bum I raised on a bottle, and because she was small and persistent, I fed her on the bottle longer than I fed my other bums. She figured out that bottles were kept in the refrigerator just inside the back door to the house, so she would wait for someone to open the door so she could come inside and beg another meal. Friendly grew up to become my lead sheep, willing to follow me anywhere, to lead the herd in the direction I needed them to go. I usually kept granola bars in my pockets, so the rattling of a wrapper could get the entire herd to head in my direction. Instead of herding my sheep from be-hind, I stayed in front so they would follow, thanks to the help of my sweet lead ewe. I'll be glad to continue her genetics, and one of her three daughters from last year is currently in the herd as well. I'd left Friendly and a few other old ewes in a pen at home, fearing they were not robust enough to lamb out on the open range this year, but per-haps in a few weeks, they can rejoin their herd. Right now, they are to-gether in a small group, eating alfalfa with not a worry in the world.

The wind is relentless this morning. It started during the night, loud enough to wake the bum lambs and make them cry out from the darkness of their protected stock trailer. During the day, I turn them out into a small pen so they can enjoy the sunshine, but this morning, they'll have to stay inside. The sheep herd is in two separate groups, hunkered down to stay out of the wind. Not much is moving, with the exception of the wind.

As I drive around the pasture, I'm pleased with the changes to the landscape I see happening since the sheep have arrived. With three years of no livestock grazing on this pasture, the soil surface had become impenetrable, with rain and snowmelt running across the surface and causing erosive gullies, rather than soaking into the earth. The hard, crusty surface that initially gave my dogs and sheep sore feet has now been churned by hundreds of small hooves as they walk and graze. Even as nimble mouths crop grass and brush, new growth is stimulated, and the cushion plant community in all its varied forms is sprouting in all directions. Small pellets of sheep manure fertilize areas the herd has grazed and bedded, able to do its nourishing job now that the soil surface is more welcoming. This rangeland has evolved with grazing, and it awakens in response to grazing pressure. We'll harvest nature's spring bounty, then move on to the next area, leaving nature to continue along without us until next year, or the year after that.

Rant stopped in at camp this morning for some food, but soon noticed ravens flying below the camp and went out to investigate. Two ewes had each given birth to single lambs during the night, and the ravens were surrounding them, causing the ewes to stamp their front hooves threateningly. Rant hurried down the hill to join them, scattering the ravens and lying down near the sheep protectively. Rena joined him later, but approached one ewe too closely and was promptly chased away. As soon as the ewes and lambs move off from their birthing area, the dogs are quick to consume the birth materials.

I've taken to shooting at the ravens every chance I get, either with my pistol or my shotgun. It would be a violation of federal law for me to kill one, and I know there's no chance I'll actually hit one, but I want the damned things to fly away when encountering a human. The poison bait that the federal agent had set out two days ago is long gone, and yesterday I was hopeful that our raven problem was on its way to being resolved, but today it seems I have no shortage of the pests, even though I have not observed them flying aggressively at the ewes. Fighting a ewe for her lamb is something we just can't tolerate from these big birds. If they're able to threaten domestic sheep protected by guardians and shepherds, I hate to think what they might do to unprotected pronghorn does, or to a brood of sage grouse chicks. Not a pleasant thought.

The relationships between wild and domestic species are often overlooked, but Europe's vultures and their reliance on domestic livestock provides an example. In response to public health concerns, European health regulations now require all cattle carcasses to be removed from fields, but this has resulted in a shortage of carrion for large birds in Spain, including the griffon vulture. Since disposal of carcasses in a transhumance system is impractical, researchers recently discovered the importance of transhumance in providing an important resource for the vultures. Griffon vultures are most common in association with transhumance movement of sheep and cattle in Spain, and transhumant cattle provide much more food for the vultures than just that available from local livestock. Other species, including bears, wolves, and eagles, benefit as well. When faced with a shortage of domestic animal carcasses, the vultures reportedly took to preying on live domestic animals.

◇ ◇ ◇ ◇

The winds did not recede today, but the sunshine broke through, putting the sheep on the move. I slowly followed, making sure that no lambs were left behind. I stood on a hill and watched as a pair of ewes that had gone to water at the reservoir raced back up the hill in a panic, bleating for their lost lambs. From my vantage point, I could see the lambs curled up in the brush, sleeping peacefully in the warmth of the sun. When the ewes approached closely enough that the lambs heard their cries, there was a mad rush as the lambs scrambled to their feet, diving under their mother's bellies for an enthusiastic tug on the milk bag.

The herd eventually made its way to Coyote Rocks, and as I walked around the back side, a shadow fell across my path. I squinted up into the sun as a large dark bird, wings stretched wide as it soared directly above, peered down at me. It was a golden eagle that had been perched on the rocks, looking out over the sheep and their guardians below. Only my arrival had disturbed the magnificent bird of prey.

A few years ago I was fortunate to witness a golden eagle hunt and grasp in its talons a young fleeing pronghorn, as a doe frantically struck the bird with her front hooves in a futile attempt to save her fawn. In a small basin about forty miles from our lambing ground, Jim and I have also observed wintering golden eagles hunt adult pronghorn—much larger prey. The eagles harass the herds until the pronghorn break into a run, becoming a spinning mass. Although we've been lucky enough to watch the chase numerous times, we've never seen a kill, but that doesn't mean one didn't occur. Many golden eagles migrate to Wyoming to winter here, and year after year we've witnessed this distinctive hunting behavior. And we've heard of other golden-eagle hunting behavior that is equally fascinating.

Naturalist Adolph Murie described golden eagles harassing bears in Alaska, swooping down and dive-bombing the bruins. Other naturalists have also viewed this behavior, with the consensus being that the eagles were either playing or curious, or simply hanging out waiting for the bears to take down prey that could be scavenged.

But a few more recent observations have provided an entirely new view of the relationship between golden eagles and bears, as detailed in a 2008 article in the journal *Ursus* by Norwegian researchers Ole Sorensen, Mogens Totsas, Tore Solstad and Robin Rigg. The article noted that in April 2004 a Norwegian research team followed a female brown bear with three cubs as they moved and foraged on an open slope. One of the cubs was smaller and slower than the other two, and repeatedly fell behind enough that the sow had to turn back to retrieve the straggler.

At one point the researchers watched as a golden eagle glided out of the clouds and grabbed the lagging cub with both feet, lifting it into the air as it struggled and cried. The mother bear's rushing charge came too late: the eagle flew over the research team as they watched through binoculars, the captured cub "struggling, its feet and head waving from side to side as it vocalized loudly. The eagle, carrying the cub, gained altitude and was lost from view when it flew into the clouds."

The team could hear the cub crying for several more minutes, suggesting the eagle had landed with its prey. The team was unsuccessful in finding the cub's carcass.

This incident raises the question of how often eagles prey on bears. The researchers posed the question to the international community and solicited several responses. There were incidents in Slovakia in 2005 of eagles harassing bears (either small bears or sows with cubs), causing the bruins to run for tree cover, dodging and evading as they retreated. In addition, a brown bear cub recovered from the Italian Alps in 2003 was confirmed as killed by an eagle.

In the 1950s a Canadian naturalist observed a large eagle carrying a black bear cub overhead before dropping it onto a rocky lakeshore, where it landed with a thump. The eagle watched it from above before retrieving the carcass and carrying it to a nest. In 2002 fragments of a yearling brown bear skull were found in an eagle nest in Poland.

The authors of the article on eagle predation on bears concluded, "Predation on bear cubs by eagles might be more common than it appears from these few observations because the opportunities for direct observations by humans are very limited." Even if it only happens every now and then, it's fascinating subject matter.

I'm both surprised and thankful that we've never had problems with golden eagles preying on our lambs, but I do believe the dogs have something to do with that. If we did experience losses from eagle predation, the problem would almost certainly have a better resolution than we've experienced with ravens. Areas with confirmed golden-eagle depredation problems can be so designated, enabling eagles to be captured and removed by licensed master falconers. The captured eagles are then trained for use in sport hunting. I've hunted with falconers using golden eagles and it's an unforgettable experience.

So much has happened, it's hard to believe it has been only three hours since sunrise. The wind finally stopped late last night, and with a bright moon, the animals were active. I had five ewes give birth next to the camp where a small herd bedded, but the main part of the herd bedded on a hillside not far away, facing Coyote Rocks. I listened to the dogs barking during the night, and knew that Rena was near camp, Luv's Girl was farther away with the main herd, and Rant was somewhere around Coyote Rocks.

When I started the morning check, I found Luv's Girl located on the south side of Coyote Rocks, curled up below about five ewes and their lambs, all born within the last day. I drove around the back side of the rocks and saw another ewe and her lambs, and Rant stood up so I could see him along the top of the rocks, but he never came down to greet me.

Since the animals were all still bedded, I decided to drive out the two-track road that is the main access to my camp, determined to find the source of the sage grouse drumming that Jim had heard the week before. As I started down the road just outside the pasture fence, a burrowing owl popped its head out of a burrow along the road's edge. I stopped to admire the small bird of prey, but it wasn't having any of my company, flying away, chattering in disproval as it left.

I bumped down the two-track along the pasture fenceline just over a mile before I spotted Jim's lek. It was a grassy opening surrounded by sage, and even this late into the breeding season (well into May) there were plenty of grouse in attendance, including hens. I enjoyed the display for a while as the sun crept higher above the Wind Rivers, then made a quiet retreat.

The pasture fence I drove along on my drive back to camp was the subject of much national interest on the part of sage grouse advocates, although I doubted if most of them could actually find the fence or even point it out on a map.

The fence was of interest because while the US Fish and Wildlife Service was considering whether sage grouse should be granted Endangered Species Act protection, a Wyoming Game and Fish Department biologist issued a two-page preliminary report suggesting that barbed wire fences pose a collision hazard to these birds. Those who oppose livestock grazing on public lands latched onto the report as another reason to rid the western range of its agricultural industry and its associated fences.

The report was based on a small research project using our pasture fenceline. It all began when two separate falconers provided incidental reports to state wildlife officials that grouse had been injured or killed on the top wire of certain fences located near important grouse areas. The range here is believed to have one of the largest concentrations of sage grouse on the planet.

According to the preliminary report, "One of these falconers subsequently began marking such fences with aluminum beverage cans in a volunteer effort to reduce these mortalities." The shiny cans would make the fence more visible and thus reduce avian/fence collisions.

The study sought to quantify the level of sage-grouse fence strikes and mortalities and test whether the fenceline could be marked to effectively reduce collisions in a cost-effective, visually nonintrusive manner. There are two large grouse leks in the area, located within just a few miles of a range fence, and the region also winters at least a few hundred grouse. The fenceline became the study area, with its three strands running nearly five miles.

In the two and a half years prior to marking of the fences, observers documented evidence of wildlife fence strikes and mortality while driving immediately adjacent to the fence. They found evidence of 170 bird strikes/mortalities and 2 pronghorn mortalities. Sage grouse accounted for 146 (86 percent) of the 170 strikes/mortalities documented. The other twenty-four observations included 4 waterfowl, 5 raptors, 2 passerines, 1 shorebird, and 12 unknown birds.

Researchers then marked quarter-mile sections of the top wire of the fence with commercial bird diverters or homemade markers that are similar to those used in other areas to reduce lesser prairie-chicken fence mortality. In the next year and a half, collisions were once again observed, with 7 grouse strikes in marked sections, and 47 strikes (36 sage grouse) in the unmarked sections. The research suggests the fence markers (all types combined) reduced bird collisions by 70 percent over unmarked sections, reducing sage grouse collisions by 61 percent.

The study is ongoing, with the previously unmarked sections of the fence being marked, and vice versa. Markers are being changed as well, with highly reflective tape added to the white markers to increase visibility in winter months.

Although we'll know more once the study is complete, what we know now is this: not every fence is a problem. Those that tend to cause problems feature one or more of these characteristics: constructed with steel T-posts; constructed near leks; bisect winter concentration areas; border riparian areas. State wildlife officials are developing guidelines for prioritizing what fences need to be marked to reduce grouse collisions, and are in the process of making markers available to ranchers at no cost.

The threat of fencing to grouse is not a new concern. Prior to the installation of fences on open range, there were no vertical obstacles protruding above the sagebrush, allowing grouse to fly unimpeded just above the shrub canopy. Grouse tend to fly just high enough to clear the sagebrush, and the birds, either not expecting the barrier created by a fence, or their large size making maneuvering to avoid a fence difficult, have occasional collisions. Sage grouse are often called "bombers" because in flight they can resemble B-52s.

Despite the impact to sage grouse in some areas, fences remain an important management tool, and not all fences are bad for sage grouse. Fences are used to ensure proper grazing use and rest for rangeland plants used by livestock.

Jim and I drove the fenceline study area last fall, and found one collision event—a sage grouse. There were a few grouse feathers on the top strand next to the marker, and grouse feathers in a heap on the road. But the grouse was gone—quick work for a predator.

What the research effort does not mention or address is that golden eagles and other birds of prey have been known to drive their prey into fences and other obstacles to injure or kill them—it's a hunting tactic. Back at the home ranch last August, I watched a grouse forced by a bird of prey to crash into a willow stand. Rant, who had also witnessed the scene, was quick to respond and ended up with the stunned grouse, which was sorry luck for the avian hunter that had orchestrated the successful maneuver. I know that some people doubt my claims that raptors will drive their prey into obstacles, but

I've no doubt it is done intentionally by these highly skilled hunters of the sky.

I returned for breakfast, and was just opening the camp door to let the sunshine in when a coyote howled to the northwest, sending all three guardians running in the same direction from their separate posts. Rena and Luv's Girl eventually returned to camp for a meal and a rest. Rant, however, was nowhere to be seen. After feeding my bums I decided to find the missing dog, and as I drove, Rena followed along behind. I headed slowly along the back side of Coyote Rocks, but no Rant. When I came around the front, Rena came over the top, with Rant giving chase from behind. *That's strange,* I thought. I shut off the truck and began picking my way up the rocks. I couldn't see Rant, but I could hear him softly crying. When I rounded a boulder, I found him lying on the ground, facing a tiny lamb curled up in the nook of a rock. The lamb was stuck, and Rant had guarded it, and had probably done so all night from the sound of his night calls and the coldness of the lamb's mouth. My heart swelled with pride for his noble work, and I gushed in praising him while freeing the lamb from its nestling place, holding it out for Rant to sniff. Rant was happy to let me have the baby, but he did follow me to the truck to see it get put into safekeeping before he collapsed flat on his side in the rocks, sound asleep. Valiant guardian, the weight of the responsibility he bears is exhausting.

Rant had been guarding a bum lamb I'd been trying to catch for days. I recognized it by its small frame and because its head was dirty from stealing milk from unsuspecting ewes. I brought it to the camp and gave it a warm bottle, but it drank little, I suspect because it

Rant naps with an orphan lamb at my camp.

wasn't flowing from a warm udder. I corralled the other bum lambs into a pen to soak up the morning sunshine, and placed the new lamb in their midst. As I went about my chores, the burros wandered into camp, and stood with their necks hanging over the pen's sides, visiting with the wee lambs. Bill gently set his nose down on the new lamb's back, blowing out softly. The burros have done that to me before, so I know how comforting it feels, being caressed like that, with warm breath and soft whiskers.

◇ ◇ ◇ ◇

That night, I woke in the darkness to the sound of a ewe chattering to her newborn lamb. This repetitious throaty murmur begins as soon as the lamb hits the ground, while the ewe cleans her new babe and encourages it to get up. I smiled as I listened, knowing a smart ewe had just given birth just a few feet outside my camp.

Daylight came with a thick overcast blanketing the western flank of the Wind River Mountains. It was another serenely beautiful morning, with subdued light and chilly temperatures in the twenty-degree range. Most of the sheep herd had moved onto the hillside at my camp to bed for the night, and this morning there were three new mothers in the bunch. A second group of sheep, the nursery group of about twenty-five ewes and fifty lambs, bedded near the Coyote Rocks, and the morning check revealed lots of activity, with lambs jumping to their feet and launching attacks on udders.

Back in camp I heard coyotes howling, with the wails coming from three directions; it appears they have us surrounded, but I'm confident that our guardian dogs have displaced them from this pasture and moved them out into the surrounding countryside.

I opened one of the doors to the stock trailer protecting my bum lamb bunch, enabling them free movement between the pen, where they can play and munch on native vegetation, and the comfort of their shelter. Their bodies are becoming nicely rounded in response to the bottles of milk I feed them every two or three hours during the day. The new lamb, initially hesitant to suck on the bottle, watched the other lambs greet me eagerly, and became inspired. The lamb, a buck, lay across my lap getting his belly full of warm milk, and turned his head to study my face as he drank, as if memorizing my features.

He seemed to be wondering why his mother looked so different from before.

Each of the big dogs stop in to visit the bums during the day, sticking their heads through the panels to sniff and lick them. Most evenings, I take the lambs for a short walk to inspect the nearby brush, burrows, and diggings, and at least one guardian dog drops by to join the walk, and then patiently waits outside as I close the trailer, putting the lambs to bed for the night.

Luv's Girl stops by to visit with the bum lambs in the pen at my camp.

Twice today I fell asleep sitting upright in the pickup truck. A disturbance inside my camp had broken the quiet during the night, and when I went to investigate I discovered a pair of white-footed deer mice engaged in a tumbling match, complete with squeaks and squeals (the mice squeaked and I squealed), taking place near the stove. The mice dove for cover from my flashlight, but continued their fight elsewhere. I tried to ignore the sound and go back to sleep, but Abe didn't like it either, placing his head on my sleeping bag, nudging me to get up and do something about the noise.

These mice put me in mind of our young burro Roo, back at the home ranch. During the summer of Roo's first year with us, I presented her with a few oats as a treat early each morning, and soon a deer mouse began joining her for breakfast. They were delightful together, eyeing each other and munching away. So last night I let the deer mice be deer mice.

Midmorning brought a spring snowfall, big fluffy flakes quickly covering the range in a layer of white. Rena rejoiced at one more opportunity to make her version of snow angels.

The herd moved south to a protected swale, while I churned up mud, making the rounds to check on ewes and lambs. Two hours after it began the snow abruptly stopped, and had soon disappeared altogether, leaving a soft steam rising over the steppe.

CHAPTER 5

guardian life

◇ ◇ ◇

Just as they do in their countries of origin, in the United States live-stock protection dogs live with their herds full-time. Most range sheep are highly social western white-faced sheep, primarily of the Rambouillet, Targhee, and Columbia breeds. Range herds, usually consisting of about one thousand ewes and their lambs, will typically have four or five guardian dogs working among them.

The dogs seem to take on various jobs according to their individual natures, with one dog serving as the lead animal, forging just ahead of the herd as it moves, while others take up position near the flanks and others trail along behind. When danger is spotted, the dogs will generally join together to confront it. Sometimes this means charging forward aggressively to ward off the threat, and sometimes the dogs will attack. The dogs confront a variety of predators, from small animals such as foxes, to bobcats and coyotes, to bears, wolves, and mountain lions, as well as aerial predators like ravens and eagles that can kill young lambs.

Henry S. Randall's nineteenth-century text *The Practical Shepherd: A Complete Treatise on the Breeding, Management, and Diseases of Sheep* describes the early Spanish sheep dogs imported to North America with merino sheep. These dogs were fierce defenders of their herds. Randall describes how "after night-fall the dogs separated themselves from the sheep and formed a cordon of sentries and pickets around them—and woe to the wolf that approached too near the guarded circle! The dogs crouched silently until he was within striking distance, and then sprang forward like arrows from so many bows. Some made straight for the wolf and some took a direction to cut off

Overleaf: Rena loves life on the range.

Luv's Girl stays close to her herd during a snow flurry.

his retreat to forest or chaparral. When overtaken his shrift was a short one."

Most guardian dogs in range-sheep operations are not pedigreed animals but crossbreeds, the result of a natural breeding system where the most fit working dogs survive, compete for breeding rights, and pass on their genetic material. Livestock protection dogs are raised with livestock from a young age, and stay with their herds night and day, year-round. They don't live in doghouses, and they seek shelter in the brush with their herds when the weather is bad.

The bitch usually gives birth to the pups in a protected space like a culvert, or under a building. We bed the pups in fleece saved from shearing, so that they will associate the smell and feel of the wool with the comfort of their mother's nest. They cuddle in the wool, chew on it, attack it, and play in it.

Once the pups are a few weeks old and their eyes are fully open, they start to venture out and are able to have their first contact with sheep. The pups are drawn to the sheep, since the sheep smell like the wool of the birthing den. Sheep are gentle creatures and smell and greet the new babes, often lying down in their presence. The pups will climb up on the sheep and curl up to sleep in their wool.

Adult ewes will discipline young dogs if they become too rambunctious, butting the pups until they lay quietly and show submission to the sheep. We also pair our young dogs with adult dogs, which model appropriate behaviors.

When the lambs go out grazing with the ewes, the pups follow, so they all grow up together. Eventually the sheep won't want to go out without their dogs and the dogs want to be with their sheep.

Contrary to popular belief, the dogs don't think that they are sheep, and the sheep know that the dogs are their protectors. The sheep also understand that one guard dog isn't the same as another. Individual sheep develop individual relationships with their protectors. Just because a particular sheep happens to like a certain guardian dog doesn't mean she'll like all guardian dogs.

The sheep also recognize that a guardian dog is different from a herding dog, and will respond differently to both. And guardians surely know the difference. Some guardians will defer to herding dogs as they work, but others will have to be restrained when a herding

dog is doing its job. Younger guardians tend to be less trusting of herding dogs, but even our most mature guardian dog, Luv's Girl, will inter-
fere with our bearded collie Abe when he tries to herd the sheep,
knocking him down on occasion.

Sometimes Jim and Cass will butcher a sheep for our freezer, but
we don't allow our guardian dogs near while the butchering is being
conducted, since this can make the dogs very distrustful of the person doing the work. These dogs have long memories and are independent thinkers, so any sin is not forgotten. As one Massachusetts
author wrote in the early 1800s about his Spanish sheep dog, "He
never forgave an injury or an insult; offend him and it was for life."

The dogs are varied in color, from white to yellow to tan to brown
with black masks. Hair coats are either short and slick or longhaired.
Some guardian landraces have thick conformation, while others are
narrower at the flank for running after predators. By definition, landraces are local varieties of domesticated animals that, through the
process of natural selection, have adapted to the distinct environments in which they live, for a specific function. Guardian dogs are
more diverse than formal breeds, since thousands of years of natural
selection in their countries of origin has resulted in the variety of
types we see today, rather than human selection for particular standards. Most of our dogs weigh about one hundred pounds as adults,
and continue growing until they are about two years old. Females are
generally smaller than males.

Every dog is different. Some dogs will range too far to be of service
to farm flock owners. These dogs are best turned over to range opera-
tors who can use the dogs in their migratory operations. Some dogs
are too aggressive. We had a Kangal female, Carolina, who would kill

any pup that wasn't hers. Some dogs will chase big-game animals such as deer, or will prey on their fawns in the spring. A few dogs will even fight to the death over breeding rights to females.

Aggressive guardian dogs pose another dilemma. Range sheep use lands also enjoyed by people for recreation—hikers, bikers, and back-packers. When strangers come in contact with the sheep herds, the dogs will confront them, not attacking, necessarily, but behaving aggressively enough that people are intimidated to the point of avoiding the flock. This sometimes leads to bad public relations. One evening a middle-aged couple pulled up to Coyote Rocks in their vehicle, got out, and began looking for arrowheads, walking among the ewes and lambs bedded there. When the guardian dogs came charging out at them from two different directions, I intervened, but I honestly don't think those people ever even knew they were targeted, or why.

Other guardian dogs may not be aggressive enough. We had a Great Pyrenees male, Tucker, who would confront coyotes and hold them back from the herd, but wouldn't bite or kill them. Some of our dogs have been so trusting that they've approached strangers, only to be stolen or "rescued" by someone wanting a big beautiful housedog. But these dogs haven't been bred to be indoor pets, so they often end up in shelters because of behavior problems. The behavior problems are only resolved when the dog is returned to its herd.

We've found livestock protection dogs to be exceptionally perceptive and sensitive, taking immediate note of changes in their environment and quickly responding to perceived threats. They will physically place their own bodies between their sheep herd and danger, be it a truck barreling recklessly down a road, or an approaching black bear.

The dogs are also highly intelligent. We've had guardian dogs hide

Hillary's position amid Coyote Rocks shows how well
the burros blend in with their environment.

Above: A ewe tends to her twin lambs. **Below:** After failing to tightly close the door to my camp, I returned from checking the herd to find it had been invaded by curious creatures.

Above: The black bear is another common predator on this range, using the river as a transportation corridor. **Below:** The corrals where we sort and weigh the lambs. **Overleaf:** Rena watches over a group of young lambs as they race up and down a two-track road, playing.

Above: A Nepali sheepherder moves a group of lambs across a grazing allotment nearby. **Below:** We raise livestock guardian dogs in close association with sheep from the time they are born so their bond is very close throughout their lives.

Above: A litter of red fox pups looks out from their natal den.
Below: Although we use a variety of non-lethal measures to protect our herds from predators, sometimes we need reinforcements, including aerial gunning of predators on our lambing grounds.

A rainbow colors the sky above the sagebrush sea and my beloved flock.

their dark-colored noses in the snow in order to evade detection (Tucker, the Great Pyrenees male, and FloJo, an Akbash female). This pair actually took pups from the house and deposited them in an empty coyote den up the draw, hiding them from us. We don't know why they exhibited this wolfish behavior.

I've watched dogs hide, laying in wait for an approaching predator, as well as stalk a predator in the manner of a lioness on the hunt. I've repeatedly tried to get a good photograph of Rant guarding his herd, but he's usually so well hidden, my attempts have come to naught.

Although livestock protection dogs have much in common, each personality is unique. Some are sweet and maternal, others are aloof, and others are downright prickly. The common factor is that they all want to protect the sheep from harm. In raising pups for other livestock producers, I've had the pleasure to live with a variety of wonderful guardians.

Tucker was nicknamed Tourista because he loved to visit other sheep flocks, traveling dozens of miles to do so, clearing coyotes out of the way as he went.

George was named after George Foreman, the boxer. He was big and loved to fight. He was an amazing dog, but during a ferocious battle with wolves in the Wind River Mountains, both his front legs were slashed, and his throat was partially crushed when one of the wolves grabbed him by the neck. George had saved his sheep, but his life would end a few months later when his tired, injured body sought eternal rest. It still makes me cry to think about our noble fighter George.

Overleaf: Rant, on guard and under cover.

Luv was a female I raised, the mother to Luv's Girl. Her name was entirely my fault. She was shy as a pup, so I would woo her in for food by gently calling, "Here, love." Jim and Cass complained they sounded like idiots when they had to call her. There's just no manly way to do it.

"Whup" was short for "Whup Ass." An almost-orange-colored female, as a pup this girl thought she was the toughest dog ever to walk the earth. She constantly attacked adult guard dogs, never quite figuring out that they were out of her league. She eventually moved over to Pete's to guard his herds, and was six years old when the wolves caught her out alone and killed her.

Juel was the ultimate mama dog. She'd mother anything and always had baby lambs mistaking her for their mother. She was patient, standing almost on tiptoe while a lamb would nose her belly, looking for an udder of milk. If she stepped away, she might knock the lamb down, so she stood still, even though that little lamb nose poking into the soft of her belly had to tickle.

Snip was the comedian. If you put anything down on the ground for just a minute, he'd run over and snatch it, racing away while looking over his shoulder, hoping to be chased. He stole the weirdest things—my work gloves, a flowerpot (with a plant in it), an air pump I was using on a bike tire, fencing pliers. Whatever he could get in his mouth, Snip would steal. Born nearly bald, he became a massive and handsome adult male.

Two normally sweet mama dogs, Juel and FloJo, found a big beaver in the irrigation ditch below the house one summer afternoon. Juel was named after the reservoir near where she was born, and FloJo was named after the athlete Florence Joyner, because she was beautiful and could run as fast as a cheetah. The beaver must have come down the ditch from the head gate at the river, a couple of miles away. For the beaver to get back to the river, it would have to hike about half a mile overland. Unfortunately the big pool in the ditch that the beaver ended up in was where all the irrigation water spilled out onto the meadow, right next to where the ewes were lambing that year. The two guardian dogs were serious about protecting the new lambs, so when they saw a thirty-pound beaver come waddling across the meadow, they were alarmed. That poor beaver looked up to see about 250 pounds of dog running at it and turned around and dove back into the ditch, swimming with all he had to get to the deep pool.

The dogs threw a fit, pacing up and down the ditch bank, watching for the beaver to surface. They could see air bubbles break the surface, so they knew the general area the beaver was in. When the beaver finally poked its nose out of the water, FloJo couldn't stand it, diving in nose-first after that beaver. It didn't do her any good—a beaver can outswim a dog any day. After about an hour of those dogs pursuing the beaver, we decided to intervene, with Jim and Cass holding the dogs back while I took a broom and escorted the beaver out of the ditch, across the meadow, and into the nearby river bottom.

We also had a young male Anatolian guardian dog, Trill. One winter day a bobcat came over the top of the ditch and tried to enter the sheep flock. Trill, just five months old and intent on proving himself, took off after the bobcat and the fight was on—up and down that river bottom. Jim and I tried to keep up with the action, but couldn't, although we could hear that cat screaming and hissing and the dog barking, branches breaking, and the general chaos of a wild fight. The cat managed to get the dog out onto the frozen ice of the river, headed toward a hole. Of course the ice broke, plunging dog and bobcat into the cold water. I swear that cat tried to drown the dog, and there was nothing we could do about it. But the dog finally won, biting the bobcat in the back of the neck and shaking it as he found a foothold and climbed out of the river. Trill was too proud of himself to know how badly he'd been wounded. It took about forty stitches to get his back sewn together, and then an infection finally killed him anyway. What a warrior.

During lambing, Rant would prove his worth as a guardian time and time again. Jim watched over the sheep for me one cold rainy night so I could have an evening at home to catch up on paperwork. The rain turned to snow, and I worried about getting back to the herd. When I called to check in the next morning, Jim hadn't been able to find Rant, but he had heard him barking during the night. I emphasized how important it was that Rant be found—for him to disappear like that, odds were that something was amiss. Jim looked and looked, to no avail. He feared that since Rant wasn't as bonded to him as he was to me, the dog wouldn't necessarily reveal himself unless he had a compelling reason. I arrived back at the herd before noon, and it took me nearly two hours of searching to find the guardian. He was stationed on a distant hillside, in the deep brush, next to the body of a lamb. Lost in the snowstorm, the babe had simply curled up, and Rant had stayed by its side, watching over it. But we did not find the guardian in time to save his lamb. Once again Rant was relieved when I took charge of the cold body. I felt that I had failed him.

Rant, a two-year-old dog from a pedigree several generations removed from guarding livestock, had quickly defined his role on the lambing grounds. When the ewes and lambs would rise from their sleeping or resting places and move off, Rant would slowly walk back and forth across that territory. If any lambs had been left behind, Rant would lie down beside them and not budge. He had determined it was his job to guard these unsupervised lambs, and it was then our job to find him and free him of the burden.

Rant, standing up to reveal his presence before
blending back into the landscape.

Rena loves life on the range. Weary in the mornings after her night-time guardian duties, she sleeps soundly during the day. By late after-noon, she's up and acting like a puppy, getting revved up for the adventures of the night. She jumps up and runs in spurts, careening around outside my camp, randomly stealing objects she sees as she dashes by. That usually includes one of my boots, with the intended purpose of provoking me into giving chase.

When Jim took his turn in camp, relieving me for a night, he com-plained that I hadn't warned him about our local singing sensation—the sage thrasher, which sits atop the sagebrush right outside my camp door and sings its long, warbling song with zest. The problem is that our neighborhood songster begins its boisterous belting way be-fore sunup. The bird's volume and persistence might win admiration on other occasions, but at four o'clock in the morning you can forgive us the urge to grab a shotgun, open the door, and restore some peace and quiet.

The cool weather continued through the final week of May, with frequent rain, snow, and wind, but most of the lambs seemed unaf-fected. The vast majority of lambs do not need my assistance, but as a general rule, it is easier for me to warm up a cold lamb than cool down a hot one, so I prefer this cool weather during lambing season. Besides, the diva in me finds long johns and Carhartt coveralls so styl-ish, I hate to put them away for the season. And the temperature typi-cally climbs as the day wears on. Sometimes I'll be sloshing through new snow in the morning only to find myself picking ticks off the dogs, burros, and my pant legs that same afternoon.

Last evening as I drove around in the rain doing one of my last checks of the day, I saw what appeared to be a ewe carcass on a distant hillside, and as I observed it through my binoculars, I saw a front leg kick. An extremely pregnant ewe was on her back on the muddy hillside. Without assistance, she would die. I raced over to the distressed animal, jumped out of the truck and into the mud, and helped the ewe roll over and right herself. She had been upside down long enough that she was now misshapen, her back flat, her sides bloated, and there were rocks embedded in her coat, which I picked out for her as she leaned on me while the blood circulation returned to her legs. I had heard of sheep dying after getting stuck on their backs, but I had never seen it before until this year. One of my pregnant ewes died in a snowstorm while on her back. I had been able to save the ewe that had gotten herself turned upside down while lambing, and now this ewe. I had associated this problem with the fatter meat breeds of sheep, but apparently conditions were right for it to affect my pregnant ewes this year. The mud certainly didn't help the situation, as all three ewes were on muddy hillsides when they became stuck.

This mud is a monster. The soil in the region is clay-based, and sufficient moisture turns it into a thick, gummy mass. It accumulates on my boots and hardens into a brick. I can't just rub it off on the brush, but must scrape it off my boots. The dogs hate it and will lie down and pick mud balls off their feet, tossing the chunks into the air.

On my last check of the sheep, I found a sweet young ewe that was obviously in a difficult labor, giving birth to a large lamb. She was on her side, and I talked softly to her as I approached her from behind, gently gripping the two tiny hooves issuing from her backside. When the ewe pushed with the next contraction, I tugged until the lamb came free, breaking its birthing sac as I laid the lamb across the ewe's front legs. As I walked away, the mama was already licking her new baby, determined to get it clean and dry, talking all the while. It's nice to feel like a winner now and then.

And speaking of winners, my neighborhood burrowing owl has found a mate. The large female is now accompanied by a much smaller male, and rather than flitting around from burrow to burrow as had been her habit, she has apparently settled into her favorite— the one in the two-track road to my camp, which, happily, doesn't see much traffic. The pair has become fairly tolerant of my intrusions, although sometimes I do feel as if my admiring glances are met with scowls. Rather than drive over her burrow, Jim and I have taken to detouring around that spot in the road to give the pair their quiet time for nesting.

My neighborhood burrowing owl has found a mate.

The pronghorn buck that initially caused me grief has remained with the sheep herd. I don't know why, and at this point I really don't care—he's just part of the scenery now. Maybe he's here because we're trespassers in his territory; maybe he prefers our company to his own. Either way, he's made no movement to join the other pronghorn bucks in the pasture.

The seasonal movements of the Sublette pronghorn antelope in western Wyoming are believed to represent the longest migration of a mammal in the Lower 48. The animals range from Grand Teton National Park south through the basin to Interstate 80. Part of this movement involves traveling through a half-mile-wide path of open land between two major rivers called Trapper's Point, a migration bottleneck west of the town of Pinedale.

Pronghorn are the fastest North American land mammal, capable of reaching running speeds of about sixty miles per hour. An antelope fawn just a few days old can easily outrun a human—but then again, so can my lambs when I'm trying to catch them.

Pronghorn are the only hoofed animal in the world to shed their horn sheaths. The horn on a pronghorn is actually a bony core covered by a stiff, hairy outer sheath that is shed annually. The livestock guardian dogs are regular collectors of fresh pronghorn horn sheaths; my yard at the home ranch is often littered with these special dog treats.

Fog can bring danger, and this morning dawn came ever so slowly. The sheep had moved in, surrounding my camp during the night, and were hesitant to move off the bedding ground in the morning's heavy mist. I trudged through the mud to check on ewes and lambs, but visibility was limited to the point that I gave up and went back to the camp to wait for the fog to lift. As the mist drifted away, opening up the landscape, the ewes and lambs slowly ventured out. Within an hour, sunshine began breaking through the clouds, but it was a game of shadow and light, with the sun eventually losing as the clouds let loose a hailstorm. Thankfully it only lasted about ten minutes, slowing into a gentle snow, but in that amount of time the storm had completely covered the ground in white. Within hours, the snow had been chased away by a rising wind. Springtime weather on this range is its own drama.

Rena accompanied me on my morning check. We got out of the truck to mingle with the sheep, and all was peaceful until a sleeping lamb suddenly jumped up and started barreling right for us. I did not want the baby lamb to get separated from the company of its mother, so I yelled for Rena to get back in the truck as I started running for the vehicle. Rena, perhaps fearing I was mad about something she'd done, was convinced I was pursuing her, and started running away from me. Anyone witnessing the event would have laughed: dog chased by human chased by eight-pound white lamb. Who knew such a tiny baby could cause such a ruckus?

Jim was spending the weekend with me and we had a leisurely evening sitting around camp. I changed into my pajamas and we went out together to do one last sheep check for the day, driving around the pasture in the protected luxury of the pickup truck. A laboring ewe was high on a hill alone, so we decided we'd better herd her toward

Rena patrols the herd in the early morning light.

my camp for the night. The ewe had a pair of tiny hoofs starting to stick out her backside.

An ominous black cloud was moving toward us, so Jim decided it might be best to give the ewe an assist. Grabbing onto the ewe with one hand, he reached around and pulled the lamb out with the other. The lamb was fine, the ewe instantly in love with the newborn, and Jim twisted his ankle in the process. Luv's Girl rushed over to see the new arrival, as did the burros, so it was quite a busy scene, with the ewe trying to make everyone leave her baby alone, the dog barking and lunging at the burros to keep them back, and the burros hurrying in with noses down trying to sniff the baby.

With the wind starting to whip up, and the ominous cloud looming, Jim hobbled to the truck, intending to bring back the stock trailer to provide the new babe some protection, while Abe and I waited with the ewe and her new lamb, keeping the enthusiastic guardians at bay. Chilly in just my pajamas and a coat, I held Abe on my lap to provide some warmth.

Jim arrived with the stock trailer just as the rain started. We put the lamb in the trailer, and the mother ewe jumped right in behind her. By then, a second set of hooves was visible, but we let the ewe take care of that one on her own. A vigorous hailstorm, complete with lightning, was pounding down as we pulled away from the trailer. We were relieved that the mother ewe with her lamb was now safe and dry, bedded in hay. The next morning, I let the new mama out of the trailer with her two ram lambs, while Jim headed home to ice his sore ankle.

The bum lambs are doing very well, with most graduating from being bottle-fed to drinking milk from a special nipple-adorned bucket. With three nipples on each side, the bucket allows me to feed up to six lambs at one time, and this bunch has taken right to it; I refill the bucket four or five times a day. They are becoming nicely rounded and spend their time either asleep or nibbling on things, tasting their world. Both Paula and Dimmy now prefer the company of their lamb friends to me and the dogs.

The prairie dogs on this range are shy in comparison to the ones in the colonies on our home ranch forty miles away. At home the prairie dogs are fairly bold, standing atop their mounds and chattering, or lounging near the entrance to their burrows, even as we walk nearby. Here on the lambing ground, I see their burrows and diggings, but only get glimpses of the small rodents as they dive for cover. I wonder if it's because the threat of golden eagle predation is higher here.

Western Wyoming is home to the white-tailed prairie dog, which lives in smaller, less dense colonies than its black-tailed cousin. There are major behavioral differences between the two species. Blacktails primarily occupy the short-grass prairie regions of the state, and occur in highly concentrated, dense prairie dog towns, projecting the classic prairie-dog-town image familiar to most people. Our white-tailed prairie dogs hibernate during the winter, whereas black-tails are active all year.

Prairie dogs weigh up to three pounds, and are eleven to thirteen inches long. Although I have a hard time seeing them out on the range, sharp-eyed Rena was fast enough the other day to catch and kill one, bringing her flea-infested prize to the edge of camp to show it off. Although Rant was impressed and coveted her treasure, I was not, and wanted her to take it somewhere far away to reduce my chance of any further encounters.

CHAPTER 6

a lovely lull

◇ ◇ ◇ ◇

Three weeks of busy lambing is followed by a lull. Instead of nine new births overnight, there are only two. The dogs are lounging around restfully near the sheep, which are fairly contained, scattered on one hillside and valley, so I can have a breather. Jim joined me once again for the weekend, bringing Friendly and the older ewes that had been left at home for the early season, along with their new lambs. They quickly rejoined the herd. Jim and I drove out to the adjacent pasture to examine the vegetation and decide what route we'll use to trail the sheep to their next grazing area. Some of the areas where there should be water are dry. It was a winter of low snow levels, and while the spring storms have been a blessing for fresh vegetative growth, they've done little or nothing for replenishing reservoirs. Instead of heading up a draw I had expected to be dotted with water holes, we'll head down, toward a natural spring, eventually working our way to the Big Sandy River later in the season, as the days grow hot with summer.

When Jim and I arrived to examine the spring and the ancient set of sheep corrals nearby, we spotted a mare and colt seeking out water. They stared for just a moment before bolting into a draw and racing out of sight. They are wild horses and they are not supposed to be in this area, which is outside a federally designated wild-horse-herd-management unit, but the mare has moved from her range to the south, stealthily shifting to new range to foal.

Although cattle and sheep ranches have reduced their herds in response to the reduction in forage available as a result of the ongoing drought in desert rangelands in the basin, wild horse populations

Overleaf: A first-time lamber cuddles with her new babe.

continue to increase. The Bureau of Land Management, charged with managing wild horses and burros on public lands, conducts periodic horse roundups, gathering the animals from the range and offering them to the public for adoption.

Most wild-horse roundups in western Wyoming occur in late summer, with hundreds of excess horses gathered and removed from arid rangelands. A contract crew runs small groups into a trap, sorting them into pens, loading them into tractor-trailers, and trucking the horses to the BLM horse corrals at Rock Springs, where they are adopted out for a small fee.

With all aspects of the roundup overseen by a BLM specialist, the horses are hazed, driven into a portable trap by a helicopter, with a tame "Judas" horse used as a lure to lead the wild animals into the pens. A crew of cowboys is on hand to ride and rope the few horses that evade the maneuvering of the helicopter. All animals are handled in a safe and humane manner.

Blood samples taken from horse herds in this region indicate that the herds are primarily derived from American saddle- and ranch-type horses, but with a significant Spanish component.

Since wild horses have no natural predators, horse populations can quickly grow to exceed the range's capacity to sustain them over the long term. Horse-removal programs are the primary method of controlling wild-horse populations.

The current free-roaming population of wild horses and burros on BLM-managed lands is estimated at more than 30,000. In addition, another 28,500 are held in either corral or pasture/refuge facilities for short-term or long-term holding. And nearly every time a roundup is proposed, someone files a legal appeal or stages a protest because

A helicopter rounds up wild horses from the western range.

they object to management and control of what they see as a symbol of the American West. We who live on the range understand that too many horses, like anything in excess, can do an extraordinary amount of damage. Rather than supporting shared rangeland, wild-horse advocates call for removal of domestic livestock herds and the ranchers who own the herds.

After visiting western Mongolia, where the relationship between man and horse is much closer than it is in the United States, I briefly contemplated America's ban on using horse meat for human consumption. I admit that I find the whole argument somewhat artificial. The Kazakhs have very close relationships with their horses, riding them daily, tending to their needs, and caring for them—their lives often depend on their horses. As a general rule, their horses are not allowed to get old and die on the range, which we know can be a miserable, slow death. Instead, the horses are killed and eaten when feebleness begins. The death is quiet and humane, and is preceded by a short blessing. It takes about fifteen goats and one cow or horse to sustain a family of four through the six months of a Mongolian winter. Western arguments against the consumption of horse meat seem sophomoric to me now, considering there are people on this earth who are hungry—that's the ethical component of my concern. Horse meat should be an option. We have wild horses overpopulating the western rangelands, yet we do not allow them to have a humane death, instead insisting that they be protected to the point that they are allowed to starve to death during the winter. Our "civilized" way of thinking is sometimes far removed from the natural cycle of life and death.

The rain, snow, and wind finally stopped, and just before midnight, it was as if a bright spotlight had been turned on and was shining through my window. The clouds had moved out, revealing a nearly full moon lighting up the night. That meant the animals were on the prowl. I could hear the dogs barking in all directions, and I could hear coyotes in the distance. I slept fitfully, worried about the nursery bunch on the other side of Coyote Rocks. I awoke once to Rena's furious barks and looked out the window to see Bill the burro approaching the camp. Within seconds I heard his hooves hitting the side of my cooler, which sat just outside the door. A midnight raid on the refrigerator! Abe and I burst out the door and ran Bill off, then jumped back into bed. The moonlight provided inspiration to our sage thrasher, which then sang to its heart's content for the remainder of what was a very long night.

It was cold, with a heavy layer of frost and temperatures dropping nearly to zero, but at least the wind and precipitation had subsided. I did the first check of the sheep early, my first concern being the sheep near Coyote Rocks. They were still bedded, but several ewes were in the process of lambing. Seeing Luv's Girl's bright white form among them assured me that all was well, so I turned my attention to the other bunches of sheep. I had been on patrol for about an hour without seeing Rant, so I decided to backtrack, returning to the girls near Coyote Rocks. At the sound of the truck he stood up from his remote spot in the tall sagebrush, wagging his tail but not moving forward to greet me. I hurried over, wrestling my leather gloves onto my hands, fearing he was once again protecting a dead lamb. But this time Rant was keeping watch over a live lamb, its umbilical cord still wet, curled up in the sagebrush. When I reached down to take it, Rant stuck his head in my way to stop me. I poked his head with one finger to scold, and then rubbed his ear to provide reassurance while I grabbed the lamb with the other hand. Rant was very concerned, sticking his nose on the lamb's side to get a good whiff. I drove the lamb to the nursery herd, but every ewe that had recently lambed already had twins, and no one was willing to claim the new lamb (which was probably a triplet) with the exception of Rant, who came running to save it again when he heard it cry. I recaptured the babe and took it to camp as an addition to the bum bunch. Rant had once again saved a lamb's life.

It was a clear and sunny spring day, and the sheep herd worked its way north of Coyote Rocks, spreading out through the pristine sagebrush to graze and nap away the afternoon with their lambs. Late in the afternoon I did a check for the dogs, finding Luv's Girl watching over a ewe giving birth. The ewe had two wobbly lambs sucking and butting her milk bag, but a third lamb had been born dead, and Luv's Girl was lying near the carcass, waiting for assistance. She was happy

Rant guarding a newborn lamb that had
become separated from its mother.

to see me, and jumped into the cab of the truck for a ride once I picked up her dead charge. When I dropped her off in the shade of Coyote Rocks, Rant came out from his hiding place along the top of the rocks to greet us. I found Rena lying in the shallow end of the reservoir, so by the time she came back to camp she was wet, muddy, and happy.

The sheep apparently enjoyed last night's mild weather and bright moon, with the herd roaming around grazing and vocalizing until two o'clock this morning. The coyotes howled, the dogs roared, the songbird sang, and I tossed and turned. At sunrise I fed the bum lambs their first milk of the day and was getting ready for my first check of the bedded herd when Luv's Girl arrived with a treat for the orphans. She had caught and killed a jackrabbit, and came running through the sagebrush carrying it to the pen, whining for me to let her in with the lambs. I did not comply. She left her offering outside the pen, and Rant guarded it for a while, but even he grew bored with the dead hare and left it for me to dispose of later. Yuck.

I took advantage of the midmorning calm to drive home and take care of some pressing correspondence. Knowing the guardians were on duty, and the sheep were content, I had no fear of leaving the herd alone for a few hours. As the season progresses, they will need me less and less. On my way out, past the burrowing owls but along the pasture fence, I encountered a coyote, for the second day in a row in the same place. The coyote was already running as I approached in the ranch truck, but I took him for a spin anyway, chasing him away from the pasture. After about three-quarters of a mile, I gave up and turned the truck back around to get on the two-track road headed for home, and as I did so, I saw a small plane flying low over the north pasture fence. I figured it was either Allen, a friend and coyote hunter extraordinaire, or our federal animal-damage-control specialists.

As I crossed the bridge spanning the New Fork River, I saw sandhill cranes in the irrigated hay meadow along the highway. The cranes signify the coming of spring each year, arriving just after our mountain

A sandhill crane plays with a piece of manure, tossing it into the air.

bluebirds return. One of the most beautiful sounds in the world to me is the rolling call of a sandhill crane from a riverside meadow.

Greater sandhill cranes come to this basin to mate and rear young, and in the spring can be seen leaping through the air with wings out-stretched, doing their mating dances. One spring I had the pleasure of watching a sandhill crane busy throwing a chunk of cow manure in the air, hitting it with his head and beak, playing with it like it was a Hacky Sack. I have no doubt that wild animals sometimes simply like to play, and their actions are reflections of joy.

Sandhill cranes fiercely guard their nests, from which will hatch one to three long-legged and long-necked downy babes. The family stays together for nearly a year, migrating together, with young always returning to the land from which they originated.

There is something entirely peaceful about cranes, and when they take to the air, the gracefulness of their trim bodies and massive wingspans is a sight to behold. My friend the talented author Stephen Bodio wrote about cranes on his Querencia blog this way: "I like it that the cranes inhabit some of my favorite places. They breed from 1,000 miles inside Siberia all the way to Idaho, winter from Nebraska and New Mexico to Chihuahua. They traverse the Bering Straits. Their rolling call, produced in a French horn concealed in their breast-bones, rains down from winter skies and haunts my dreams."

Crane fossils about ten million years old have been discovered in Nebraska, indicating that cranes are our oldest surviving bird species, haunting the dreams of generation after generation.

Once at the house I hurried to take a shower and send off my email, arriving back at camp in less than three hours from the time I'd departed. Two strips of florescent-orange and white-checked flagging draped across the sagebrush greeted me at the door to my camp. It was the federal pilot's calling card, letting me know they had flown over the sheep this morning hunting for coyotes near sheep herds in the area. I called the gunner and soon learned that the crew had shot nine coyotes between my camp and Pete's ranch. I told them what direction I would soon be headed with the herd, so they could fly that area in their travels as well. Things were going well for my herd, but I learned that another herd nearby had forty-five lambs killed by snowstorms and coyotes in the last few weeks. I'll continue to count my blessings, including the excellent guardians I live with. We just might make it through the season in fairly good shape.

Some people chase coyotes with greyhounds and other sight hounds in a sport called coursing, but one warm late winter afternoon at the home ranch, I tried it using sheep guardian dogs. From my seat at the writing desk, I watched a coyote approaching near the ranch buildings, causing the two young guardian dogs kenneled there to erupt into frantic barking. I stepped out the door and set two-year-old Rena loose. She ran toward the coyote, slowing as she got closer, and saw that the animal had its hackles up and didn't appear friendly. Rena kept looking back toward the house as she tried to figure out what to do. She was a young dog then, unsure of herself, not having had any experience with coyotes and with no adult dog to teach her the rules, so she proceeded slowly. Once she started to get a little aggressive, forcing the coyote to run, I released Rant, at that point just a big male pup, not quite a yearling. He flushed a second coyote, and then all the canids disappeared into the dips and folds of the mesa above the ranch. After about half an hour I went to find the dogs and met them just as they came off the south end of the mesa a mile away.

They were happy but obviously unsuccessful at killing a coyote—a good first encounter for inexperienced young dogs. Had they been successful, they would have returned bloody and battered.

My husband's cousin is one of the proprietors of a wool shop in Dubois, Wyoming, located on a scenic highway en route to Jackson Hole. Once a timber town, the forced collapse of the timber industry devastated the small community, but it has re-created itself as a tourism destination. With about one thousand residents and a majestic mountainous backdrop, it's the place to go for uninhibited snowmobiling in deep powder in the winter, and for a variety of outdoor recreational pursuits in summer. Now it's also the place for niche shops targeting the tourist trade, and the wool shop is a popular stop. The shop is a cooperative venture undertaken by a group of local women, and sells locally produced wool yarn, soaps, blankets, and clothing. It is just one example of the economic bonus that can be associated with pastoralism in any corner of the world. The products of transhumance vary from milk and meat to specialty products such as soaps, craft items, and clothing.

Transhumant nomads in Iran make up only 2 percent of that country's population, but supply a major portion of its milk, meat, and wool.

Handicrafts created from transhumance livestock systems are a staple of the economy in Mongolia. Camel felt rugs, sheep's wool outerwear, and cashmere hand-combed from goats and made into luxurious sweaters and hats are popular items. Local artisans peddle their wares at community festivals, museums, and shops frequented by tourists, and a specialty shop is located in the capital city of Ulaan-baatar. The Tsagaan Alt Wool Shop, a nonprofit, sells fine articles that are made by disadvantaged Mongolian women.

In India's Johar Valley, the Bhotiyas are a tribal people who have traditionally practiced transhumance and gathered rare wild Himalayan herbs. They maintained a specialized breed of sheep and goats, large animals that could be used as beasts of burden in addition to their wool, meat, and milk production. But political policies resulting in a decline in transhumance, including the severing of trade routes with Tibet, have brought about big changes for the Bhotiyas and for the region. The number of sheep in the valley has been reduced by 80 percent, and wool production has fallen off substantially, with a subsequent decline in traditional handicrafts and wool weavings. The variety of crops produced in the valley has declined as well, a result of the lack of trade options.

Fine wool from range sheep in transhumance systems in the western United States is used to create dress uniforms for our nation's military, and is also sold to Italian fashion designers. Although many farm flocks in the United States produce sheep that are primary meat breeds, range sheep are wool sheep, with meat a secondary market.

Rant earned his keep yet again this morning. The sheep were bedded in two groups, and when they moved out to graze, the guardian began his systematic walk through the bedding area while I went about my chores. When I returned to the herd I saw him stand up, watching me, wiggling his butt frantically. He'd found something—a big skinny lamb with a dirty head. The lamb was one of two that had been

A newborn lamb rests in the sagebrush, well hidden from view.

bummed for one reason or another; I'd been trying to catch them but had failed thus far. The lamb was nosing into Rant's belly, looking for something to nurse from, and Rant was calmly waiting for me to save him. Having collected Rant's find, I finally ran down the other skinny bum, bringing my bum-lamb pen population to eleven.

That afternoon, as I was lounging in my camp reading a book, Rant came to the open doorway and peered in. That was unusual, so I went to the door and saw that he was being tailed by one of the bum lambs, which had escaped the pen. I laughed and grabbed the lamb, securing it in my camp while I heated up milk for the orphans. The lamb agitatedly paced around inside the camp. I thought it was just hungry, but as I was preparing the bottles, it threw itself to the floor, twitching and thrashing around in some sort of fit. It would get up

again, walk a few paces, and then repeat the performance. If I didn't
know better I would have thought it had been poisoned. When I had
the bottles and bucket ready, the lamb refused to drink. I placed it on
the ground outside and it followed me to the pen. I then turned my focus to the other ten lambs, and when I turned back, number eleven
was gone. *Hmm.*

I looked for the lamb as I walked back to the camp but it was
nowhere in sight. Placing the now-empty bucket and bottles inside
my door, I walked farther afield and could soon hear the babe returning my calls of "Lamb, lamb," from the deep sagebrush a short way's
off. The wayward lamb had followed Rena this time, and the dog was
seeking the shelter of taller and thicker brush in an attempt to get
away from its thrashing. I retrieved the lamb once again and had it follow me back to the pen. As I leaned over to place it back inside, I spotted a big yellow-and-black bumblebee resting on the ground within
the enclosure. *Aha!* Not poison at all, but a bee sting. That explained
the bum's strange behavior. It soon recovered from the painful sting.

It's the second warm, windy day in a row, and the level of our small
reservoir, the main water source for the herd, has dropped drastically.
When I did my rounds in the afternoon, I spotted a lamb stuck in the
heavy clay mud of the reservoir, unable to pick up its feet to move. I
got out of the truck and waded in to lift the lamb to shore, but when I
tried to move, I found that both my feet were stuck as well. I pulled
and pulled, pulling myself out of my right boot first, then my left. I
ended up having to shed my socks and pants before making it out,
muddy, tired, and irritated. I knew it was going to be dirty work, rescu-

ing the lamb, but I hadn't known how dirty. Performing a tug-of-war with each article of clothing still in the muck, I managed to get all of my clothes out as well, although I had nearly given up on my left boot when it finally came free, sending me reeling over backwards, landing on my butt in a slightly drier patch of mud. I walked barefoot through the sagebrush, carefully placing each foot so I wouldn't step on cactus, carrying my muddy clothes and boots, and, as it turned out, drawing the attention of a yearling ewe. She wandered over to check me out, spending much time examining my muddy legs and toes before I found a bag of potato chips in the truck to distract her. Behold the power of salt.

The lambs spend their days running around in gangs, racing back and forth on hills, digging in loose dirt, bucking, bouncing and leaping, butting heads, and sproinging on all four legs, stiff-legged. Typically a small group will start a stampede, picking up more lambs as they run, until it's a continuous wave of lambs racing back and forth, back and forth. Their mothers cry for them to come back and behave, but are ignored. If a ewe comes over to try and retrieve her lamb, she could end up with a gang of twenty hoodlum lambs aimed at her udder, so the ewes pretty much stand back to do their complaining.

Lambs, like human babies, love to chew on things, and will put most anything in their mouths, first sniffing, then pawing, then chewing. From vegetation to the wool on other sheep to the ears of other lambs to fences, lambs nibble as a way of getting to know their big new world.

Lambs resemble pronghorn fawns in some ways as well. If I sur-

Overleaf: A pack of lambs races back and forth.

A pronghorn antelope doe tends to her three fawns.

prise a lamb without its mother nearby, the lamb will curl up and try to melt into the ground, making its outline as small as possible, exactly what pronghorn antelope fawns do to hide from predators. In this way the lambs "go antelope."

◇ ◇ ◇ ◇

Dawn again comes slowly, with heavily overcast skies threatening the landscape below. Late in the morning, the wind picks up, swirling and whistling as a snowstorm settles into the basin. It may be June, but the storm works its fury until falling silent as darkness descends once again.

The first people of European ancestry to explore and make use of this region were those associated with the fur trade in the early 1800s.

The Wind River Mountains were rich in beaver, and mountain men including William Sublette and Jedediah Smith explored and trapped in the region in the 1820s. The annual mountain-man gathering known as Rendezvous took place up until the 1840s, when changing fashions ended the demand for beaver.

Beginning in 1843, emigrants began traveling west over the Continental Divide along what would become known as the Oregon Trail. They used old trapper routes such as the Sublette Cutoff, which is just a few miles east of my camp. As the number of emigrants increased in the following years, the trail west was improved to become a wagon road. It was Wyoming's first government-financed road, taking 115 men ninety days to construct at a cost of less than $70,000. It was completed in 1858, and was named the Lander Road in honor of the man who surveyed it, Captain Frederick W. Lander. Serving as a shortcut for emigrants headed to Idaho and the Pacific Northwest, the Lander Road branched off the main stem of the Oregon Trail just west of South Pass, and rejoined it in Idaho. The route saw three hundred wagons a day, and tens of thousands of travelers with their livestock came through here every year, for three decades.

The trails that traverse this sagebrush sea are called the Oregon Trail, California Trail, and the Mormon Trail, but here where the wagon ruts are such a familiar component of the landscape, they arc collectively called the Emigrant Trail. This is the first of the lands of the original Oregon Territory those emigrants would see, having just traversed South Pass, crossing the Continental Divide. Although this land seems remote and nearly uninhabited today, as if untouched by humans, nearly four hundred thousand settlers traveled Wyoming's Emigrant Trail in the mid-1800s, on their way to Oregon and California. About one-tenth of the travelers never made it, but died along the trail, usually from disease such as cholera. Their gravesites are common along the trail, heaps of stone serving as their only markers.

As I walk with the sheep, listening to their gentle murmurs and clipping of the brush and grass as they graze, the guardian dogs approach alongside me, bumping against my legs in gentle greeting. As we walk, with my hands caressing the big dog heads at my sides, I wonder about my shepherd brethren around the world. In our thousands of miles apart, are we having the same experiences? Are they greeted in this way by their guardian dogs, and do they, as I, enjoy hearing the sounds of a herd of ewes and lambs as it moves as one? So many shepherds throughout the world use livestock guardian dogs, and I'll wager they have as strong a connection to their animals as I have to mine. It's a certainty that their connection to the natural world in which they live is deep.

William Adams wrote in 2004 in his *Against Extinction: The Story of Conservation,* that the conservation challenge ahead is not preservation or restoration, but to reconnect humans with the wild, to reestablish our human relationship with nature. Without such contact, Adams maintained, the human ability to understand nature, and to engage with it, withers. He wrote, "The future of conservation will turn on the extent to which a strong individual connection to nature and natural processes is maintained."

The reservoir having dwindled, it's imperative that the herd be moved. With Abe's help, Jim and I began an early-morning push to the next pasture, intent on showing the herd their new water source before allowing them to graze freely. As we trail the sheep, they stream out across a ridge and down a long draw. We use two prominent landmarks to guide our flow over the land, keeping Pencil Point and Tabernacle Butte in sight as our navigation points. Both buttes stand at higher than 7,200 feet in elevation in this undulating landscape, dwarfed by the nearly 7,900-foot Elk Mountain that rises between them. Elk Mountain is a monolith on the horizon here.

We work hard for seven slow hours to trail the sheep to the new camp and to its new water source. The sheep want to move up, and it's

Abe the bearded collie loves the job of moving the herd.

a job to force them to move down the ridge, down the draw. Baby
lambs tire easily and want to nap, not keep trailing.

We move several miles to take over a grassy ridge, with a natural
spring in the draw below for the sheep to water. The view from my
camp is now many square miles of high desert rangeland.

Just upriver from the new locale is a place called Buckskin Crossing, which commemorates the home site of trapper Buckskin Joe and
his family, who lived there in the 1860s. This site was a common crossing of the Big Sandy River used by trappers and mountain men, and
later became a ford for the Lander Cutoff of the Oregon Trail and the
thousands of emigrants who traveled that route.

Although historic signs along the trail note that all that remains to
show the passing of thousands of emigrants across this landscape is
the deep ruts from wagon wheels and the graves of those who didn't
survive the journey, I see other indications of their legacy. All of the
trees along the trail were cut down for use as fuel, and the herds of
oxen, horses, and mules wiped every blade of vegetation from along
the route. Different plant species more resistant to grazing now grow
in their place. With all other options gone, the emigrants eventually re-
sorted to sagebrush for fuel. From the trail we can learn that the composition of plant species in a landscape is always related to the
grazing presence of animals, regardless of whether the animals are
wild or domestic.

The view out the living room window at our home ranch is a rich
panorama bordered by Ross Butte and Ross Ridge, located across the
New Fork River from our home. They are a pair of high mesas covered

in desert cushion plants, low grass, and big sagebrush plant communities. The area doesn't experience much use other than the grazing of livestock. But it is an amazing place—home to ten rare plants and nine regional endemics. Grazing isn't a concern for these species, since they are of compact stature and low palatability. One of my favorites is one that grows nowhere else in the world—the Big Piney milkvetch, which is abundant in the area and covers the ground in tiny purple flowers. A member of the pea family, it's a mat-forming perennial herb with flowering stems less than three centimeters high. It is always associated with sagebrush and cushion plant communities, and quickly recolonizes disturbed sites.

The Wyoming Natural Diversity Database (once part of The Nature Conservancy, now affiliated with the University of Wyoming) considers the Ross Butte/Ross Ridge area one of the most significant botanical areas in the state. This is sagebrush country, not forest or grassland. The shrubs provide essential forage for domestic livestock and wild grazers, as well as cover from weather events and predators, and concealment for birthing. Many of the sagebrush plants on this range are more than one hundred years old, dear old friends.

Lake Gosiute was an ancient deepwater lake that covered most of the basin during the Eocene. As it receded, it left an opportunity for the evolution of a new kind of sagebrush, a variation of the Wyoming big sagebrush. Wildlife seem to prefer this sagebrush to other types, as western Wyoming's thriving pronghorn antelope, sage grouse, and mule deer populations amply demonstrate. As widespread as sagebrush is across the western landscape, so little is actually known about this plant community. The description of the botanist W. W. Bailey, writing in an 1870 *American Naturalist,* still rings true: "After careful inquiry I am led to the conclusion that no one has ever seen a young sagebrush . . . All the specimens met with, and their name is legion, look as if they had been produced, not only mature, but aged: as if they are coeval with the mountains and plains upon which they are found."

Desert plants like sagebrush have developed a process in which parts of the plant die and shed, allowing the remainder of the plant to survive and produce new growth. Although most grasses have shallow root systems, sagebrush (and other hardy native vegetation in the sagebrush community) have a fibrous root system near the surface, in addition to a deep taproot system that reaches twenty to thirty feet below the surface to the permanent water table. The mean annual precipitation for this range is only seven or eight inches a year, with more than half of that in the form of spring moisture in April, May, and June. A sixty-day frost-free growing season is about the most one can expect.

In cold desert shrub or semiarid conditions like this sagebrush steppe, moderate livestock grazing over the long term results in a decreased density of vegetation, but increased productivity of individual plants. During periods of stress caused by drought and extreme temperature, plants of grazed areas are more likely to survive than those in nongrazed areas. The nutritional content of the native vegetation makes it highly desirable as a food source. The amount of digestible protein is higher in bud sage than in alfalfa hay. Western Wyoming is a very good place to graze sheep.

It began a little after midnight. I could hear Rant barking and raising a ruckus for what seemed like hours; he was either tangling with something or preparing to. The battle sounds kept coming closer, climaxing at around 2:30 A.M. outside my camp window. I looked out into the darkness to see Rena and Rant and a third figure, and when I grabbed my flashlight and hurried out the door I found Rant and another canine upright on their hind legs, brawling. When I got closer I realized that the intruder was Rant's brother Turk. The two stud dogs had not seen each other since they were puppies, and Rant was guarding what he viewed as his territory. Turk, part of a migratory sheep outfit by now, also viewed this range as his.

I hollered at the dogs, and that was enough for them to release each other and drop to the ground. Rather than retreat, Turk crept forward slowly with his head down, looking to the side in a gesture of subordination. Despite Turk's submissive body posture, however, Rant attacked again. But Turk was both brave and persistent in his attempts to come closer.

Rant calmed down a little when it became apparent that I was glad to see the visitor, but he was still determined to keep Turk away, from the camp as well as from me. I backed off, hoping to defuse the situation, and Turk stayed in submissive mode while continuing to insist his presence be allowed. That was all right by Rena, who greeted him enthusiastically.

It soon became evident that Turk wanted to check out the lambs in the bum lamb pen. Rant would have none of it, keeping his body

---

Overleaf: The herd rests during a midmorning move.

between Turk and the pen, lying down facing his brother. Knowing this stud-dog standoff could go on for hours, I went back to bed.

I arose before the sun to find Rant and Rena lying in the sagebrush just outside my window. When I stepped outside to greet them, Turk sat up to reveal himself nearby, initiating another attack from Rant. I was most definitely off-limits to the visitor.

Turk stayed in the area throughout the morning, but kept his distance from the camp so as not to further provoke Rant. I tried to make peace between the dogs by driving out to Turk and petting him, but Rant was not appeased.

Midmorning, Rena erupted into furious barks, and I could hear dogs and coyotes in the big sagebrush draw below my camp, toward the spring. She and Rant took off to investigate, and I waited to see what would happen. I was very surprised when a third large guardian dog came out of the brush. This was another intact male guardian, accompanied by a smaller adolescent pup, apparently sired by Turk, from the looks of her. These dogs did not come toward my camp, but were busy hunting coyotes in the draw near the spring. Eventually all the dogs turned their attention to the hunt.

When I went to take a closer look at the two newcomers I recognized the large male as Bernard, whom I'd raised as a pup and had trained in the same lamb pen with Rant and Turk. Rant and Turk were littermates and lived together until they were five months old; Rant and Bernard had shared a kennel together for a few weeks when they were three months old and first getting bonded to orphan lambs. Rant had not encountered either of these two male dogs since that time—at least a year and a half. The dogs were all the same age—two years old, all unneutered males, all about twenty-eight inches at the shoulder.

After the coyote quarrel, the three visiting dogs went to check out my sheep herd and were greeted by Luv's Girl, who was also familiar with the two adult males. The sheep, spooked by the new dogs, flocked around Luv's Girl for protection, but soon settled down when she remained calm, regarding them as fellow guardians. The burros had also known Turk and Bernard as pups, and gave only a toss of their heads in warning in response to the adolescent female pup's brief but boisterous barks. The dogs stayed with the herd for a few hours before returning to a hillside near my camp for a nap.

Turk made another attempt to check out the lamb pen, and was promptly disciplined by Rant. I inspected him later, once Rant had completed the lesson in manners, and found both of Turk's front legs had puncture wounds, his ribs had been raked on one side, and one side of his face had been bitten by Rant. None of the wounds was severe; Rant was simply out to make a point. Turk did not fight back, but submitted, acknowledging that this was Rant's camp, that Rant was the boss.

Perhaps thinking he'd have better luck, Bernard paid a visit to the camp, but Rant proved just as inhospitable, and Bernard quickly backed down.

I called Cass to see if he could shed any light on the visiting dog pack, since he was working for Pete and, because of his skill with animals, was often giving the task of dog wrangling. He explained that the dogs had come from two different sheep herds miles away, in two different directions. A wild animal had been "screaming" near Pete's

Rant postures to keep Bernard and Turk away from my camp.

ranch during the night, and the dogs all went crazy in response, he said. A mountain lion had killed a calf above the ranch the previous week, consuming about half the carcass and peeling the hide off, and everyone assumed it was the lion that had once again set off the dogs during the night.

My visiting dogs had joined together and were traveling across the landscape in a hunt for predators, much as a pack of wolves would do in seeking out prey. According to Cass, my herd was the third herd they'd visited, with their jaunt to my camp ranging from three to ten miles.

My sheep herd, with Luv's Girl and the burros, moved down to the spring midday, and the visiting dogs slept in the sagebrush nearby throughout the afternoon. Rant stayed close to camp and his lamb pen, keeping the other dogs away.

When I went to feed the bum lambs in the evening, the visiting pack took it as an opportunity to try to invade camp. I turned around to see Rant and Turk rise on their hind legs, at each other once again, open-mouthed, grappling with their front legs, while Rena took Bernard to the ground and mauled him into submission. This was the first time Turk had fought back, and Rant finished the match with a sore front shoulder, but the visitors once again were forced to retreat to the sagebrush below camp.

Rant wasn't too put off by the fights. When I finished feeding the lambs, he hurried over to lap up the remainder of the milk and waited while I cleaned the buckets, wagging his tail and playfully falling over onto his side, soliciting my attention. He was actually in a pretty good humor. Rena was not. Luv's Girl had simply shrugged off the territorial dispute as so much stud-dog nonsense.

At dusk, the three visiting dogs joined Luv's Girl back in the hills with the herd, leaving Rant to guard his lamb pen, and Rena to her nightly patrols. Early morning found all the guardians at their stations, but later in the day, the only remaining visitor was Bernard.

Just as lambing is winding down in early June, pronghorn antelope fawning goes into full swing. There are pronghorn does scattered throughout the sagebrush, in ones and twos, each seeking a quiet place to give birth. This morning I saw a doe with two fawns, and when the little ones saw me, they dropped to the ground to hide. But they were dark brown forms against a light-gray sandy hillside, so their attempt to conceal themselves wasn't very effective. No matter, because by the time I passed by again a few hours later, they were up and running alongside their mother.

Pete called to tell me he'd found an owl nest in the abutment to a wooden bridge spanning an irrigation canal, so, taking advantage of the herd's midday rest, I drove forty miles south to have a look. A great

A Swainson's hawk perches on a fencepost.

horned owl flew from the bridge when I arrived, and when I walked down to the water's edge I could see two downy chicks scowling from their snug nest.

The irrigation canal moves water from the Big Sandy Reservoir to the Farson farmland below. I traveled the region's back roads, admiring the lines of massive hybrid poplar trees that farmers had planted as windbreaks years ago. They are the only trees in this sagebrush sea, and at this time of year they are full of nesting Swainson's hawks. These birds nest directly above farmers' houses, preying on small mammals in fields and along ditch banks, and make their presence known in the form of loud shrieks to any who would disturb them.

On my way back to camp, as I drove across the allotment's Waterhole Draw, I disrupted a nesting killdeer, which then performed its broken-wing act in an attempt to draw me away from its nest. This is the birthing/hatching season in the sagebrush landscape, and everywhere you look, it seems, there is new life.

It's hard to fully comprehend the number of hooves that have moved through this sagebrush steppe, be it the thousands of pronghorn that pass through twice a year, for thousands of years, or those of the domestic sheep herds that have fed this nation for just a few hundred years.

During the Mexican-American and Indian Wars of the 1800s, troops routinely moved through this region with their meat supply marching alongside, on the hoof. Regiments heading to wilderness outposts often brought sheep or purchased some along the way to feed their soldiers.

Westbound Mormon settlers arrived in Utah with their small sheep flocks in 1847. Later on, both gold seekers and California emigrants trailed sheep through this route, and it was estimated that nearly a quarter of a million sheep traversed Wyoming from 1847 through 1856 in westward movements.

The 1860s brought the era of the Great Sheep Trails in the West, with bands of three thousand to seven thousand sheep trailed east from California and Oregon to Rocky Mountain mining camps and Nebraska feedlots. According to Charles Wayland Towne and Edward Norris Wentworth's *Shepherd's Empire* (1945), from 1865 to 1880 the trail bands were mostly breeding stock for ranchers in and beyond the Rocky Mountains; and from 1885 to 1901 the majority of the trail sheep were bands of wethers destined for the slaughter market in the East. Those hooves trod the same ground my sheep herd now tramps. The New Fork River near our home is the site of the river crossing used by thousands of sheep more than a hundred years ago. What a sight that must have been, three-thousand-head bands of wethers making that dramatic crossing! The herds would leave the West Coast early in the spring, reaching Wyoming by midsummer, and trail across the state to arrive in Nebraska or Colorado feedlots by November.

At least fifteen million head of sheep were driven east during the Great Sheep Trail era, which ended around 1900 when stock was more easily loaded onto and transported via railcars than trailed great distances. Wyoming began the new century with an inventory of five million sheep within its borders, but only a tenth of that number remain today.

It is a very quiet morning as I venture out for a walk in the peaceful minutes before dawn. Pete's sheep are trailing through a few miles to the south of my camp, on their way to mountain pastures for the summer. Their presence aggravates the geese nesting in the tall grass near the river, and I can hear their raucous complaints from miles away.

Usually arriving before winter has ended, the Canada goose is one of the first migratory bird species to signal the coming spring in this basin. Their hardiness is apparent as they prepare to nest despite the spring snowstorms and blustering winds. Geese graze on vegetation, consuming anything from grain in agricultural fields, to flowers and roots, to seeds and berries.

Wyoming sits in the path of two major goose-migration flyways: the Central and the Pacific. Many of the big birds winter in the United States and migrate north to summer breeding and nesting grounds in the Canadian arctic and Alaska.

Although most Canada goose populations are migratory, the creation of park-like open spaces adjacent to small water bodies in urban areas has resulted in a growing number of resident goose populations in the Lower 48. According to federal wildlife officials, no evidence presently exists documenting interbreeding between Canada geese nesting in the United States and those subspecies nesting in northern Canada and Alaska. The US Fish and Wildlife Service estimates that there are 3.5 million resident Canada geese in the United States.

We often see geese migrating in their typical V formation, which provides a drafting effect for the birds behind the leader, allowing the followers to expend less energy during long flights.

During the summer molt, the birds take to the water for safety. The molt, which can last for up to five weeks or so, is a risky time for geese. Since their wing feathers are replaced all at once, they can't fly during this time. That's why they seek refuge near large expanses of open water, and in this area, it's the Big Sandy Reservoir, located downriver from my camp.

North America's largest flying bird, the trumpeter swan, has also become a regular resident of the tristate corner of Montana, Idaho, and Wyoming. Although not listed as an endangered species, trumpeter swan populations were decimated in the past and have made a long, slow return to healthier numbers, with the Upper Green River Basin becoming a key area for this expansion. I see them every summer, with their elegant white bodies and graceful curved necks, gliding along in calm waters in quiet glades.

Trumpeters were once distributed throughout North America, but were nearly exterminated in the early 1900s by trappers and market hunters who sought their feathers and skins to meet the demands of the fashion trade of the day. Swanskins were also sought to make powder puffs. Skylar Hansen, in his book *The Trumpeter Swan: A White Perfection* (1984), wrote that Hudson's Bay Company records showed that between 1823 and 1880, about 108,000 swanskins were sold in London.

By 1933, only sixty-six trumpeters inhabited the Lower 48. Most of these resident birds were found in the tristate area of the Yellowstone region of Wyoming's northwest border with Idaho and Montana. A separate population nested in Alberta, Canada, and migrated to Yellowstone during the winter, where thermal springs left open water during the winter months.

Trumpeter swans are a majestic presence in the valley
during the months with open water.

Due to extensive recovery and enforcement actions, trumpeter
numbers greatly increased, to about 450 adult birds in the Yellowstone region by the early 1950s. One project that can claim credit for
the recovery is the Red Rocks Lake National Wildlife Refuge in southwestern Montana and its winter feeding program for the swans, established in the 1930s. Half of the wintering swans were associated with
the artificial feeding program. The combination of a change in the
feeding program and the removal of about four hundred adults,
cygnets, and eggs for release in other areas took its toll on the tristate
population, but numbers climbed again by the late 1980s.

The resident tristate population also faced increased competition from the Interior Canada swan population. According to Wyoming Game and Fish Department figures, migrant numbers increased from two hundred swans in 1975 to more than two thousand in the 1990s.

While the Canadian migrants are capable of dramatically increasing their numbers because of the vast amounts of vacant spring and nesting habitats available to that population, resident trumpeters had a competitive disadvantage: many didn't migrate at all, even to available seasonal habitats nearby. Year-round resident swans were forced to meet the high-energy demands of breeding seasons with limited early-spring habitat. The result was that 50 percent of the Wyoming swans' production was taking place in just seven nest sites.

Natural resource agencies thought drastic action was called for, so in 1990 the Idaho Fish and Game Department and the US Fish and Wildlife Service (in charge of managing federal refuge lands) began hazing, or trying to scare away, wintering swans from Idaho's Harriman State Park, and captured and relocated more than 1,000 birds. The winter-feeding program was abruptly halted in 1992 in an attempt to get the swans to move in more natural patterns with the seasons, rather than relying on an artificial feeding program for survival. This combination of factors resulted in a reduction of wintering swans in the area, but the resident swan population dropped from 505 in 1990 to 246 in 1993. The termination of the winter feeding program affected as many as 200 resident swans, increasing mortality, disrupting pair bonds, and decreasing production.

Swan-restoration efforts were already well under way in Wyoming. By 1986, a captive-breeding facility had been established near Jackson, using birds from the tristate flock. Each breeding pair in the flock would produce a clutch of eggs, which was taken away and replaced in the nest with a wooden egg. The clutches were then artificially incubated.

Meanwhile, the trumpeter hen, faced with only one egg in her nest, would produce a second clutch. This is called "double clutching," and results in the doubling of the number of young produced. The young birds from the first clutches were raised for a time at the captive facility, in a pen near other broods and adults that schooled them in the ways of being a swan.

Once the cygnets were about three months old, but still unable to fly, they were moved into holding pens with surrogate-parent birds in the Upper Green River region. Within a few months, the cygnets would mature enough to fly from the pen, and when open water would start to freeze with the onset of winter, the birds would make their way south down the Green River.

Birds released in the Upper Green reestablished trumpeter-swan migration routes to wintering areas in southern Wyoming, southern Utah, southwestern Colorado, northern New Mexico, and northern Arizona. The emergence of this migration pattern should help ensure survival of the species in the future.

One June morning, I drove along a two-track road on the allotment and came over a hill to surprise two magnificent golden eagles, which lifted heavily off the ground. Curious about what had attracted them to the spot, I walked through the sagebrush and found the remains of a pronghorn antelope fawn. The hips and hind legs were all that remained. I wondered about the impact of eagle predation on fawns in areas with abundant eagle populations, and I'd wager that not much is known about the subject.

It was Jim's birthday, and Cass had a day off from his ranch job, so we all met up at home to have dinner together. Things were quiet with the herd and I knew that they did not require my presence every minute, so I was comfortable journeying home for a night with my family. Rather than worry about Rena trying to follow me out, I'd take her with me. I'd arrive back early in the morning, attending to my duties as usual, with the rising sun.

It was raining when I left the camp after the lambs' last feeding of the day, with Abe and Rena riding along with me. The rain continued throughout the night—the first night in seven weeks that Jim and I slept together in our own bed. Cass had to be up at 4:30 A.M. to head back to Pete's ranch, so I got up to get the coffee started and saw both men off to their jobs. Then I took a quick shower, loaded up my canine companions, and took off down the highway in a steady light rain. By the time I turned off the pavement, heading for the range, it was an all-out downpour, with water running down the tracks of the dirt road and into the depressions alongside it. I hoped for the best and plunged forward, knowing the lambs were depending on me for food. It was a harrowing drive and I was relieved when we finally bounced and slid our way through Waterhole Draw and headed up the hill on the way back to camp. My relief was premature, however. It took about six tense tries for me to get the truck up over the crest of the hill, and from all the clanking and grinding, I was afraid I might ruin the transmission. We finally made it over the top and headed toward camp, which was now in sight a few miles in the distance. About a half mile out, the road switchbacks through a deep draw, and I stopped the truck to take a look. The draw was running water—a small stream had appeared since my leaving the evening before. I decided to leave the truck where it was.

Rena, Abe, and I trudged through the mud as the rain continued, with thick gumbo accumulating like heavy weights on our feet. Rant came out to greet us with a guardian bark, and the lambs started calling for their morning milk as soon as they heard my voice. I had no idea where the sheep herd was located, but I was betting they weren't thirsty.

Opening the door to my camp, I was greeted with the welcoming scent of vanilla—an open bag of lamb milk powder has the most comforting aroma. I got the propane stove started and soon filled lamb bellies with warm milk and sent them back to the shelter of the big stock trailer. I returned to camp to read a book, listen to the raindrops hitting the tin roof, and watch the puddles of water grow larger outside my window.

I was lucky to have made it nearly all the way back in the truck. The steady rain continued, and I put in a quick call to Cass to make sure he had made it back to Pete's ranch safely. He told me that all the irrigation ditches had been damaged by the rainfall, six bridges had been washed out in the neighboring county, and the National Guard had been called out to help deal with the consequences of the flooding. Yet here was I, stranded in camp, with plenty of supplies, my animals healthy. All in all, things were good on my end.

The rain finally let up in the afternoon, and eventually a bright sun went to work warming the earth and making the air feel muggy. I unwisely decided to traverse the muck via dirt bike in an attempt to

Ewes and lambs move to new grazing range.

check the sheep herd, which I could see grazing on the hillsides a few miles to the northeast. Of course the bike promptly became mired in the gumbo, and I had to abandon it and trudge out once again on foot. I walked for several miles with mud-weighted boots, checking the lambs, only to find I wasn't needed; the herd had managed just fine without me. It took another hour to slog back to camp. With my truck on the other side of the draw, and my bike disabled in the brush, and even walking a near-impossible effort in the mud, I finally got it through my hard head: give it a rest; best to stay inside and let things dry out. Sunshine would eventually resolve my transportation problems.

In the North Gondar of Ethiopia, herders take only indigenous breeds of cattle on the transhumance route, with crossbred cattle being left behind. Natives believe that the crossbreds would not be able to tolerate the high temperatures, disease load, and long trekking distances endured by native livestock on the route.

A specialized local breed of cattle travels the transhumance route in the French Pyrenees. The Gascon cow is well adapted to harsh and changing weather conditions, with its dark hide and muzzle providing resistance to sun exposure, and thick black hooves allowing it to trek long distances without problem.

Native Americans in the American Southwest have long been subjected to governmental intervention with respect to their livestock. For the Navajo, the small Navajo-Churro sheep is part of their cultural heritage, although numerous efforts have been made to eradicate or "improve" the breed. In the nineteenth century, when the United States government ordered the Navajo people to reservations, to further weaken the tribe it also ordered frontiersman and government agent Kit Carson to rid them of their sheep herds. Fortunately a few sheep remained and were eventually used as seed stock to regrow herds, but a 1934 national stock-reduction program had the federal government in the business of slaughtering entire livestock herds in response to a national glut on the market. The eradication of the Churro herds was part of this effort, although many Navajo herd owners were not made aware of that—all they knew was that their herds were slaughtered and the carcasses buried in pits, with little of the meat saved for use. As a result the Navajo-Churro was threatened with extinction. But in the 1970s environmentalists working with traditional herders founded the Navajo Sheep Project to restore Churro herds. The program has been successful in raising numbers and ensuring species survival. Each year, the Navajo hold a celebration of the sheep, with ceremonies to bless and protect the herds. Like my Kazakh friends, the Navajo also conduct a ceremonial blessing before each sheep is harvested for food. The Navajo are working to keep the traditions of their ancestors alive in the modern world, and the Churro is central to that effort.

Sheepherder Louise Turk wrote about the national herd-reduction program in her autobiography *Sheep!* (2001), giving a firsthand account of what she remembers happening in Wyoming in the 1930s. Turk describes a perfect storm: a severe drought had taken its toll; livestock were starving; there was a glut of livestock on the market; and people were struggling through the Great Depression. A government-operated cannery in Sheridan, Wyoming, processed salvageable meat to be distributed through the relief program, and a government-sponsored tannery in Casper later processed the 11,517 cattle, 340,644 sheep pelts, and 595 goat skins from animals killed in the state, with a payment of fourteen dollars per head for cattle, and two dollars for each sheep. It was better than letting the animals starve. The sheepskin-leather bomber jackets worn by fliers in World War II were also a result of the program.

On Rocky Mountain rangelands, most sheep are not purebreds, but are commercial flocks of what is generally called western white-faced sheep. Ranches that are a century old have developed their own bloodlines and lineages, bringing in new rams each year, but rarely purchasing ewes. These closed flocks are exquisitely suited for the range, and for the transhumance trail, as they have been bred for it generation after generation. These are strong sheep, large in body size, growing a long wool staple, and with strong hooves to carry them along the trail.

The sunshine did indeed eventually dry up the soggy rangeland, allowing me once again to get out on foot to check the herd. A successful outing it was not, however. After failing to initiate life in a lamb that had been born dead, getting covered in blood and birth fluids in the process, I proceeded back to camp for a break only to hear a faint squeaking from the storage area under my bed. The sound, I found after tearing the bed apart, was coming from a nest of baby mice. Ugh. After relocating the nest to a spot well outside my sleeping quarters, I washed my hands (several times), but couldn't seem to get clean, especially as my jeans were stained with blood from the earlier incident with the dead lamb.

And then there was Bernard. Rant was still keeping the visiting guardian from camp, so I decided to take some dog food up to him at his outpost near the herd. Minutes after feeding him, I felt an aggressive pinching of my skin under the shoulder strap of my bra, which was followed by another, and then another. I frantically scratched, trying to find and kill the culprit, thinking that perhaps a spider had fallen into my shirt collar. The agony continued, to the point that, standing near the herd in the sagebrush, I whipped off my shirt, quickly followed by my bra. And there was the source of my discomfort: on the inside of my bra strap was a tiny, nasty, wiggling flea. Dammit, Bernard! All the other dogs had just been sprayed for fleas, so it was the new guardian who'd been the bearer of this particularly irksome gift. I put my shirt back on, tossed the bra on the floorboard of the truck, and drove back to camp for the flea-and-tick spray. I then single-mindedly stalked the dogs, mercilessly taking them down for a good drenching of spray, expending the most strenuous of my efforts on Bernard.

Walking back over the draw to retrieve my truck, I then proceeded to drive away from camp, traveling for nearly an hour just so I could take a hot shower in my own house. It was wonderful. Twenty minutes later, I was back behind the wheel, headed toward camp, rejuvenated and refreshed. Well, I was clean, anyway. What can I say? Sometimes a woman just has to do what a woman has to do.

The sheep spend their days leisurely grazing, moving to new hillsides to explore forage every few days. By their nature, they prefer open, high ground, grazing along ridges and hillsides where potential threats can be seen from a long distance. While the sheep graze, the dogs, which have stood guard all night, barking threats into the darkness, sleep somewhere close, either amid the herd or nearby.

As the herd moves, burros Bill and Hillary follow along, and will not move forward until all the sheep have gone before them. They are quiet and calm, blending into the landscape around them. They move

---

Overleaf: The ewes and their lambs seem to prefer high ground, where threats can be seen from a distance.

slowly and deliberately, and seem wise. Lambs run under their bellies and bump into their legs at play, as the burros stand serenely, not daring to lift their hooves lest a babe be injured.

It has been so wet that the rangeland continuously erupts with fresh growth, virgin flowers blossoming and new buds sprouting. The herd has settled into a pattern, and is free from my herding or direction. Most days, the sheep stay on their bedding ground until the sun rises and begins to warm the earth. Each ewe rises and stretches, standing to let their lambs fill their bellies with warm milk before slowly walking forward and beginning to graze in the coolness of the morning. The lambs surge forward to play, nibbling on this and that as they move, forming their own small herds among the wide scattering of the ewe flock. By midmorning, the herd stops to rest, and spends the rest of the day unhurriedly grazing, with an afternoon siesta and cud-chewing session during the heat of the day. The sheep graze again in the cool of the evening, coming together as the herd moves to high ground to bed.

I check the herd throughout the day to be sure all are content, but leave them to their peace, and their constant guardians. I drop off food for the dogs, or the dogs take turns visiting the food bowls at camp. The lambs are chunky and growing well, bounding out from their mother's sides to play with others, but returning to the comfort of the ewes' warm milk bags a few times a day. The native wildflowers are now in full bloom. The sheep love them and when they eat the blooms, their breath smells fresh and wonderful.

I suspect that some animal-rights advocates would object to my family's lifestyle, since it doesn't conform to their rigid standards of animal treatment. We do all that we can to provide pleasant lives for our animals, but life on the range is not without risk.

Death is a risk we live with every day, because we are intimately connected with the cycle of life, and death is a part of that. Death is something we deal with. It isn't something we're afraid of. West Nile Virus killed several of our sheep over the years; my dogs kill coyotes fairly routinely; wolves kill our dogs on occasion; and on occasion, we have dogfights that result in injury and even death (though rarely). We humans on the ranch experience daily risk as well, be it from lightning strikes, the hazards of working with machinery, predator threats, horse wrecks, and hormonal cattle—just to name a few.

We have working partnerships with our animals—they aren't simply pets, here to enhance our lives, although they do that as well. We live with and depend on one another, in various ways. My relationship with the guardian dogs isn't just about me. Livestock guardian dogs by their very nature are independent animals, so they get a vote. More often than not, the dogs decide. I try to influence their decisions, but I know I'm working with an animal that has survived for thousands of years by making its own way.

Our livestock guardian dogs lead natural lives. The males that win breeding rights, in the process of natural selection, get to breed. The females pick where they will den up—we build hay houses and other whelping boxes, but the females decide. The result is that some of our litters are born in dirt dens dug out of a hillside, others in culverts, others underneath buildings, and even a few in the designated hay houses. The females that use the hay houses seem to know what we're about as soon as we begin constructing them. We feed the female atop the house for several weeks before whelping, and they usually begin nesting and making it their own just before having their pups. The females always have the pups by themselves, and I've only lost a few from being rolled on during the birthing process. Most of our litters include eight to eleven live pups.

The pups are never locked in, and I simply can't resist touching them from the time they are born. If it's a big litter, I supplemental-feed the babes with a bottle of milk replacer. Within a couple of days of birth, the bitches usually wait for me to arrive for babysitting duty before they exit at a run, headed for water and to empty their bladders and bowels, then hurrying back to the pups. I try to line the natal dens with wool, and some females allow that, while others kick it back out as many times as I put it in. No matter—mama decides and the babies do just fine. We provide hard dog food, soaked in milk replacer, before the pups ever open their eyes.

The babies start coming out of the den as soon as their eyes open, meeting their first sheep and getting butted when they try chewing on ears that don't belong to them. They grow and venture out farther, tangling with porcupines, digging up prairie dogs, harassing moose for better or worse, chasing off magpies and hawks, and meeting up with their first coyotes and foxes. The pups have wild adventures and seem to be truly happy animals. They usually have their first coyote or fox kill while they still have their puppy teeth. And mercy, but they are proud when that happens.

The pups bark and growl all night long, roll on dead things, and stink to high heaven sometimes. They swim in the river when and if they want. They steal fish from ospreys.

Most pups survive, but some don't. We had a moose kick a pup in the chest and break its sternum a couple of years ago, and another died of an infection from a wound down its back that was inflicted by a bobcat that tried to enter the herd. We spray for fleas often because, with our prairie dog populations, we have an unlimited supply.

I socialize the pups by getting them to come to my voice, or to my whistle. I play with them, get them used to collars, leashes, and cables, and take turns taking them for rides in the cab of the truck. That way, it's not so traumatic when they have to go into the vet's office in town. They slobber and puke, have stress-induced shedding, but they generally survive civilization, only to gleefully jump out of the truck when they're home and head back to their herd.

The dogs don't live in doghouses, even in the bitter cold of winter. They will not leave their sheep, no matter the conditions. They curl up to the wool bodies they protect, fan their tails over their faces, and wait out the storms. The sheep don't use buildings, but seek out the shelter of sagebrush and natural landscape contours for protection, and the dogs go along.

Our livestock guardian dogs live very active, adventurous lives. I feed them well, providing nutritious dog food and meat on the bone. The dogs love me, but prefer their herds. They rarely die of old age. Wild animals rarely do. They live lives of bravery and I am privileged to get to share in that life with them. I mourn their passage, and I am thankful for the time I've had with each one.

Animals such as these are good for my soul.

CHAPTER 8

trails of the past

◇ ◇ ◇ ◇

Just a few miles from my camp along the Big Sandy River is a place of historic importance to the sheep industry, and as I gaze up at the Wind River Mountains, I can see the Silver Creek drainage, and realize another historic place is located there. Neither of these sites brings pleasant recollections.

The first site is an ancient deadline domestic sheep were not to cross, and it ran from the head of the East Fork River in the Wind River Mountains, following the Big Sandy River to a desert wash called Yellow Point, and all the way across this wide valley to what became Deadline Ridge in the Wyoming Range Mountains. The second location is the site of the Raid Lake sheep massacre. Both places were part of the range wars between cattlemen and sheepmen.

My neighbor Jonita Sommers wrote a book, *Green River Drift: A History of the Upper Green River Cattle Association* (1994), which describes the deadline, which is not far from my home ranch. She wrote, "The ranchers took a workhorse cavy of twenty to thirty horses to the head of Reardon Draw. By using a walking plow and switching men and horses every thirty minutes, the line was completed to the Big Sandy River in two days. It is said they scattered poison fruit on the north side of the line so that if the sheep crossed the line and ate the fruit they would die."

Wyoming's vast open and unregulated rangelands attracted great herds of cattle and sheep for grazing in the early 1900s, so many that tensions increased between resident cattlemen and what were viewed as tramp sheepmen. Many of these sheep outfits were migrants not based in Wyoming, but trailed in for grazing, eating the

Overleaf: The herd moves toward the setting sun.

grass to its roots and failing to pay state taxes. The cattlemen attempted to keep the sheepmen out, designating deadlines upon which sheep were not to cross. So began the sheep and cattle range wars, with masked riders arriving under the cover of darkness to burn wagons, shoot herders, and club sheep to death. It was estimated that at least sixty men were killed between 1893 and 1903 in such conflicts in the West, and Wyoming was no stranger to these conflicts. Although the Johnson County range wars in northeastern Wyoming are some of the most famous, mostly because the massacres that happened there turned the public against the cattlemen, several lesser-known conflicts occurred near where my camp is located today.

Sheepmen in southwestern Wyoming leased every other section, or square mile, from the railroad for their herds to graze the Red Desert, so their claims to grazing rights were well known, but as the herds headed north toward the mountains, problems arose. Cattlemen with established ranches along major waterways in the valleys didn't want sheep encroaching upon regional rangelands, even the high alpine areas above timberline where the cattle were not grazed.

Late in 1894, cattlemen in the Big Piney area learned that sheepmen were planning to move their flocks from along the railroad up into the upper Green River Valley. On April 10, 1895, a meeting of cattlemen was held in Big Piney to discuss the matter and decide upon a boundary line between the cattle and sheep ranges. The deadline was determined, and both sheepmen and cattlemen agreed to the range division at a meeting a month later.

But within a few weeks, the deadline was violated. According to *America's Sheep Trails* by Edward N. Wentworth: "Four or five flockowners combined to cross the mountains, with a dozen armed guards for protection. The cattlemen organized in Pinedale, and when the flockowners had been lulled into security by the absence of threats, attacked each camp with an overwhelming number of masked men. Herders were blindfolded and tied, and the raiders spent the whole night clubbing sheep. In each camp the equipment was burned, and about two thousand head killed. The captured sheepmen were sent back over the Bridger passes with their riding animals and a handful of food."

Raids took place throughout Wyoming, with sheepmen murdered and thousands of sheep killed, and in 1902, a massacre of sheep took place in the mountains above my camp. It was reported that grass was at a premium that summer, and ungrazed areas were practically nonexistent.

Five bands of sheep from Utah, and several bands owned by a local outfit, Joseph Thompson and Sons Sheep Company, were grazing in the South Fork area of the Wind River Mountains. The bands became intermixed and had to be sorted in a set of corrals that had been built just for that purpose. The cattlemen had gathered the night before at the Steele Ranch on the East Fork near Boulder, and it was a group of about 150 masked men who rode into the South Fork area, bound to do harm to the sheep. The sheep belonging to the local man, Thompson, were released from the corrals, but the cattlemen soon took to clubbing, shooting, and knifing the Utah sheep to death. Amid the chaos of the scene, the Thompson sheep also became subject to the massacre, and the herders were beaten and tied up. A herder was killed, at least two thousand sheep were slaughtered, and the surviving sheep were scattered into the surrounding mountains once it became clear that the cattlemen couldn't drive the herds to their deaths in what would become known as Raid Lake. A few sickening photos of the aftermath of the massacre remain in historic archives—dead sheep knee-high in a corral. The bones of the slaughtered sheep littered that ground for decades. A herder downstream from the massacre, at Poston Meadows, killed himself, fearing the raiders would come for him next. Another herder who had been tied and blindfolded later went blind, and was convinced that the dirty blindfold used on him was the cause. The identity of the raiders was never made public, although many cattlemen knew who was involved, and Thompson and his family recognized some of the faces, despite the masks.

One of the raiders later met with a fatal accident after an argument with a sheepman at Sheepherder's Delight, a bar and store located on a sheep ranch owned by Sam Leckie, near the Big Sandy. Other incidents befell other raiders, but the historic records are inconclusive, so one is left to wonder whether these were merely accidents or accountings for past wrongdoings.

No sheep herds crossed the deadline in the next few years, and the Great Sheep Trail drives were, anyway, ending. In 1905 the Forest Service was created and the Bridger Forest named (later becoming the Bridger-Teton National Forest), placing summer grazing under a controlled and permitted system, and eliminating for the most part the reasons for the earlier conflicts. Within just a few years, local cattlemen who had seen their herds devastated during killing winters tried their hands at sheep raising, and were soon petitioning the government to allow some of their grazing permits to be changed from cattle to sheep. The passage of the Taylor Grazing Act of 1934 effectively brought regulation to other rangelands in the West, ending the livestock grazing free-for-all and stopping most grazing use by transient sheep outfits.

The trail we recently walked with our sheep took them from the Leckie pasture down the Big Sandy to the area abutting the Boundary allotment, part of that old grazing deadline. History is alive in this land, as these place names attest.

I spend the late days of June feeding the bums and taking them to graze, monitoring the herd nearby and walking the hills and draws, exploring this expanse of rangeland, observing life forms that might normally have escaped my view, the tiny ants whose mounds aren't even as large as a quarter, the huge wood-ant piles that are several feet in circumference. The rust-red and florescent-green lichen that cover old bones and rocks are as strikingly beautiful as the sparkling white glaciers visible on the skyline above them. The massive brown branches of the ancient big sagebrush plants embrace this landscape in their firm grasp. I watched the dogs catch and eat jackrabbits, and laughed as Rena and I flushed a brood of sage grouse chicks from the path before us. Yes, there is much to see here, and so little time to get to know it. Days, months, years, human lifetimes, are so small in the context of this living landscape. Days such as these—peaceful and conflict-free—give me a measure of confidence in the future. The herd is doing well, and the dangerous days of lambing are now behind us. I am hopeful that we will be able to celebrate when we tally the ledger pages this fall, that we will be able to look forward to yet another season on this wild range.

Groups of lambs congregate in the early morning light.

As the weeks pass, we are slowly moving toward the Big Sandy River, where we will remain during the heat of summer. There can be danger along the river, and it can come from a variety of sources. A member of the herd could get stuck in the mud near the waterway, a lamb could wash downstream in a swiftly flowing section of water, predators may be lurking in the willows, and porcupines may be skulking around in the trees.

Adjusting metabolic rate to maintain its body temperature, and sporting a thick furry undercoat, the porcupine is supremely adapted to handle the cold winter temperatures of the Green River Basin. The porcupine is the second largest member of the rodent family found in North America, second only to the beaver. I've had my share of porcupine encounters—and so have my animals.

One bright June day a few years ago, a National Public Radio reporter from Denver arrived at our home ranch to do a story on livestock guardian dogs. I introduced him to the bum lambs at the house, and then we loaded up into the ranch truck to head out to the lambing ground.

Once in the field, we went to see the puppies at the camp I had established on the range we used that year. It was an ideal place for puppies; they were free to sleep and play underneath my camper and around a set of portable pens erected nearby, just a few hundred yards from the New Fork River. As we approached, the puppies came running in from the river one by one, with porcupine quills stuck in their noses, mouths, and paws. I sat down on the ground and began pulling quills, while the reporter, Jeff Brady, watched, took photos, and taped the event. He felt bad for the puppies, but I think he enjoyed the real-life aspect of dealing with guard animals as well. He spent three hours with me, and ended up doing a great piece on NPR. This was Luv's Girl's litter, and Rena was one of those quilled pups. After that initial porcupine encounter, I found myself having to remove a new batch of porcupine quills from a few of those same puppies several days later. Apparently we had a few slow learners in the bunch. Thankfully, they must have been tangling with a young porcupine, as the quills were fairly soft.

Porcupines do not throw quills when threatened, but the quills detach when touched. Quill tips have backwards barbs that move the quill further into tissue, making extraction difficult.

One spring, we had a ewe give birth to two lambs, early in the season, and during a snowstorm. It was evening, and she was near the ranch corrals, but we loaded her and her lambs into a stock trailer so they would be sheltered overnight. Jim threw some alfalfa hay over the back door of the trailer for the ewe to munch on, and we left for the night. When I returned in the morning to check on the ewe, I was flabbergasted to find she had porcupine quills stuck in her front legs, but there was no porcupine in the trailer, and her lambs were fine.

Each litter of guardian dog pups encounters porcupines at some stage
of the growth process, and the memory of painful quills
is (usually) enough to prevent repeat performances.

Apparently a porcupine thought it would join the ewe in her alfalfa dinner, but got stomped by the ewe, which struck with her front feet to keep the animal away from her lambs. The porcupine had managed to climb back out of the trailer, leaving a trail of quills to tell the story.

A porcupine has extremely long claws on both its front and hind feet to enable climbing, and porcupine footpads have a pebble-like texture that is used to increase friction against tree trunks or, in our case, the slick inside wall of a livestock trailer. Backward-pointing bristles on the underside of the tail serve to prevent the animal from sliding backwards while climbing.

Porcupines do not travel well over snow, and many hibernate for the winter, although some may stay out. Jim and I once had to escort a beautiful young porcupine through the sagebrush and back into the river bottom to keep it out of range of our dogs.

During the fall breeding season, male porcupines will fight each other over territory, and often they fight to the death. Seven months after mating, the female will give birth to one fully developed baby. The baby weighs about one pound and has soft quills that dry and harden within hours. The mother will nurse the baby about four months. Since young porcupines can't climb well, the baby will stay hidden near the base of a tree during the day while the mother sleeps in resting trees. The pair comes together at night, with the baby learning from its mother where the good locations are for denning, hiding, and foraging. Dangerous to curious pups (and hardheaded adult dogs), these are handsome and interesting creatures. I love seeing their beautiful, bear-like faces, which they tend to keep hidden.

✧ ✧ ✧ ✧

Though rarely seen, black bears are a common species in western Wyoming, and our expanding predator populations also include the grizzly bear, the largest predator inhabiting the basin. Yellowstone-area grizzly bears are distinctly different from grizzlies in other populations in several ways. This bear population has a high reliance on meat from large animals in its diet, compared with bears in most other populations that consume higher percentages of plants, insects, and fish. In addition, the Yellowstone bear population has been separated from other bear populations for at least one hundred years, so it is genetically distinct.

In 2007 grizzly bears in the Yellowstone region were officially removed from federal protection, after a recovery program exceeding thirty years, although a legal challenge restored their threatened status in 2010. The Upper Green River region is located more than twenty-five miles outside the official bear recovery zone, but grizzlies are now somewhat common in the region.

In 1975 the grizzly bear population in the Yellowstone region was less than two hundred and largely confined to Yellowstone National Park. Biologists estimate the population has increased to about six hundred animals, many of which make their homes on the six national forests surrounding Yellowstone. The expanding bear population has been emerging from their mountain habitats and into lower-elevation rangelands and farmlands of western Wyoming.

I prefer predators of a smaller stature. One day while I was working around the corrals, I saw movement from the corner of my eye, and curious what creature might be watching me, I dropped to the ground to sit and wait. Soon a pair of sparkling eyes peered out from underneath the wooden box used as a grain bin. It was a least weasel, the smallest mammalian carnivore in the world. Although up to ten inches in length, these miniature meat-eaters tip the scales at a mighty three-ounce maximum. The weasel watched me for several minutes as it busily moved around for a better view. The creature had moved into my grain bin, keeping the mouse population trimmed down and saving my grain in the process.

Western river bottoms serve as attractants for wildlife, drawing large animals such as bears that use the vegetative cover to move about without detection, but we also get elusive white-tailed deer, and huge moose that seem to fade into the shadows.

Since we live in mule deer country, observing a white-tailed deer is

Two white-tailed does spar over territory.

special. The white-tails that inhabit the willow-covered river bottoms along the New Fork River during the winter are rather shy and secretive, so it was a real pleasure for me to watch a dominance dispute between two does unfold one afternoon.

One doe apparently wanted the group of deer to move away from where they were grazing, but another doe wanted to stay. The first doe reared to display dominance, making the other deer move off. The herd wasn't moving quickly enough, so the dominant doe continued to rear, striking the other does with her front hooves. The doe that wanted to stay briefly put up a fight, but eventually the dominant doe won the dispute and the herd moved off.

On occasion I encounter moose along the New Fork River, but not often in this Big Sandy drainage, since it's lacking many willow thickets. Our Shiras moose seem to be living dinosaurs—on the threshold between two worlds, and perhaps on the precipice of extinction. The Shiras is the smallest species of moose on the planet, and western Wyoming may be its last, best place.

The Wyoming Game and Fish Department maintains that Shiras moose entered the state from Montana and Idaho, noting that there is no archaeological evidence of moose in the state prior to the 1800s. Moose populations began to inhabit the Wind River Range in the 1930s, and wildlife managers transplanted moose from western Wyoming to establish populations in other areas of the state.

The Shiras subspecies is named for the naturalist George Shiras, for his early 1900s discovery of moose in the Yellowstone region. Back then, the moose was described as a nocturnal inhabitant of the dark woods, but no more. Moose in Wyoming are found in drier areas than other moose populations, and are closely associated with willow

When Bill and Hillary tried to steal a calf moose,
they enraged the calf's mother.

communities, which appear to be on the decline. Today, there are about ten thousand Shiras moose in Wyoming, found in widely distributed but low-density populations, and the population trend is on the decline.

Wildlife managers have a list of reasons for concern with the basin's moose population: low reproductive rates, habitat declining

in quality and quantity, and predation from an expanding wolf population.

We have frequent moose encounters at our home ranch, usually with moose living in our winter haystacks. They often browse the willows along the river, so the sheep and guardian dogs are used to seeing them as well. The burros are often involved in encounters outside winter season, leading me to suspect that they are the instigators of contact.

One fall day Jim and I arrived in the pasture to check on the burros only to find a mad cow moose chasing Bill and Hillary. As we drove in, we realized that there were actually two cow moose chasing the burros, which had been trying to get to a moose calf that apparently belonged to one of the cows. The burros were in big trouble, and we laughed as we raced the truck over to get into the middle of the ruckus. I inserted the truck between the burros and the pair of moose to shut the conflict down. The moose cows stood sulking in the willows, watching me feed stale bread to my burros, which were very excited by the exploits of the afternoon. We suspect the burros were trying to steal the calf. The two troublemakers had had a really good time.

Another time, Jim and I arrived back at the sheep pasture in the afternoon to find quite a standoff in progress. Two young bull moose were in the pasture, but the three burros were lined up in a row, forming a border between the sheep herd and the moose. The standoff had apparently been going on for some time, since there were a couple of magpies perched on the butt of one of the burros.

These two moose were well known in the sheep pasture. They had been lurking around on the other side of the river, watching me do chores, peeved that the dogs wouldn't let them into the haystack. The dogs usually leave the moose alone, as long as they keep their distance. The day of the standoff was just another day in the neighborhood, and the moose finally went on their way into the next pasture.

There are plenty of legends and stories about what wonderful and loyal companions burros make—miners and shepherds of long ago talked to their beasts of burden and treated them like old friends, which they often became. I'm rather partial to the ancient story of

how the image of the cross came to be on the burro's back. I think of
it often, especially when I see the sheep are peaceful, in the company
of their sweet burros.

Some say the cross mark on a burro's back is a sign of God's love.
In the story of the Crucifixion, Jesus rode a burro to Jerusalem. The
burro wanted to carry the heavy cross for Jesus, but was not allowed,
so he followed Jesus to the hill of Calvary. His heart filled with sorrow,
the burro was unable to bear to watch the horrible scene before him
as Jesus was nailed to the cross. The burro turned his back, but stayed

The cross mark on the burro's back is the subject of legend.

nearby Jesus on the cross, and heard Jesus pray for those who had harmed him. To reward the sweet beast, the shadow of Jesus on the cross fell across the burro's back and remains there to this day, a visible symbol of God's love.

With that story as part of my life, how could I not simply adore these kind, brave creatures? Pastoralists all over the world know the devotion of these animals.

As the days grow hot in summer, the hillsides erupt in pink beauty—the rock rose, or bitterroot blooms. The bitterroot is a completely nondescript presence until it blankets the sagebrush steppe with its colorful spray, ranging from white to bright pink. This year the landscape is honored with deep pink flowers. Although delicate in appearance, the bitterroot is actually a succulent plant, with carrot-like roots that provide for water storage, allowing the plant to thrive in desert or semidesert regions. The bitterroot was once an important food source for Plains Indians, who dug them up in the spring and peeled and boiled the roots before eating them.

Birds that nested earlier in the season are now tending to their broods, as my recent trip to the spring revealed. The spring is surrounded by a high-walled earthen reservoir, so I never know what animals I'm going to meet up with until I come over the top of the reservoir. Yesterday, it was a half-dozen killdeer chicks scurrying around on the ground, wading through water on their long legs, and generally making the two mothers that accompanied them very nervous. One of the females took to the air, flying close to my head as she let out a shrill call, while the other engaged in the broken-wing ploy. I apologized to the harried mothers and quietly withdrew, laughing at the trouble I can get myself into without even trying.

Late one afternoon the wind picked up and the skies turned threatening, and I arrived at the spring to find one of the killdeer hens hunched down, with six extra legs sticking out from her wing feathers. Three of her babes were huddled underneath the hen, seeking shelter from the weather. Although I'd seen domestic chickens do something similar during a rainstorm, I was pleasantly surprised by the sight of the eight-legged hen at the spring.

Near the spring is an ancient water trough, turning my thoughts to days gone by and the shepherds who passed through here so many years before with their herds. About sixty feet long and sitting just a few inches off the ground, the wooden trough was lined with tin, and it stood at the perfect height for sheep to access. The sagebrush has long since grown through and around the trough, nearly concealing its presence, and soon it will disappear into this landscape entirely.

On my way back to camp after the final check of the sheep for the day, tiny sage chicken chicks scurried from the path before me. Although it's July, some sage hens nested earlier in the spring and their chicks are now adolescent-sized, so the steppe is populated with various-sized grouse chicks, some barely larger than a half-dollar. My encounters with them are sudden and short, but they leave me smiling nonetheless.

I spent several hours pushing the sheep herd into new territory in the pasture yesterday. It was very hot, with temperatures in the seventies, and the sheep came to water late in the afternoon, so I took advantage of that to push them up into the hills to the southeast, toward the river in the distance. These scalding days at high elevation will

Sagebrush is gradually reclaiming the wooden water trough.

drain the reservoir and spring where the sheep currently water, so I need the herd to be in a position to trail to the river very soon. Once the sheep herd finds the river, with its cold, abundant water, we won't graze these high rangelands any longer, but will drift along about eight miles of river, browsing nearby hillsides and range as we try to stay away from mosquitoes and biting gnats, for the remainder of the grazing season. Cass came by the camp to visit late in the day, so I sent Bernard, our visiting guardian dog, back to the ranch with him. Cass would drop him into one of Pete's herds within the next day or two.

The movement into new territory is always somewhat dangerous when it comes to predation. Pete points out that his herds are hit the hardest during the first few days of trailing into a new area, until the guardian dogs have sufficiently taken over, displacing local predators. As dusk fell last night, the three guardians disappeared into the folds of the steppe, leaving my camp strangely quiet. It was very hot during most of the day and my bum lambs had stayed in the shade of the stock trailer rather than grazing, so I had left their pen open in case they wanted to venture out in the cool of the night, under the big moon. I hadn't been asleep for thirty minutes when I heard two coyotes barking just outside my camp. I shot out of bed, grabbing the flashlight, and hurried to the lamb pen. The lambs were safely inside, so I closed it up and proceeded to fire up the truck and turn on the spotlight. The ruckus soon had Rena, and then Rant, appearing out of the darkness. I could hear Rena's deep huffing long before I could pick her white body out in the spotlight, sounding like a monster as she moved aggressively through the brush and back to camp to guard the lambs. Luv's Girl remained with the main sheep herd, as did the burros, but Rena and Rant charged around throughout the night, circling out from camp, barking their warnings, daring the coyotes to show themselves. Their calls were not returned.

The early-morning check revealed the sheep herd lounging on the side of an abandoned oil-well drilling location. According to the well marker, left by Husky Oil Company, the dry well reached its total depth of 12,944 feet in October 1973, after four months of drilling. Just another artifact left behind on this range, attesting to those who have come before.

◇ ◇ ◇ ◇

The sheep have a fairly predictable routine during these hot days of summer. For a wool breed like our Rambouillet, seventy-five degrees is terribly hot. They arise just before sunrise, grazing their way downhill toward water, heading back to the hills before the heat of the day sets in, seeking a high spot that catches breezes and blows pesky mosquitoes away. They are in little danger during the day, since the lambs are now too big for ravens to target, and most predators will only try to take a member of the herd under the cover and coolness of darkness. The burros stay with the herd, but during the hot part of the day, the dogs are often found sleeping in the shade of my camp. In late afternoon, the sheep will move around to graze for a few more hours, finding a bedding ground just before dark. The dogs will rejoin the herd at dusk, and the cycle continues.

The bum herd, too, has its schedule. I feed them a three-gallon bucket of lamb-milk replacer in their pen at dawn, noon, and dusk, and their grazing takes place on the hillsides immediately adjacent to my camp. The bums monitor my activity from afar; if they see me come out of my camp with a bucket, they rush headlong at me hoping it's time for milk. They nearly knock me down in the process, and I must push them out of the way as I wade through them on the way to the pen, where the buckets with nipples await filling. I lock the bum herd in their pen just as it's getting dark, freeing the guardian dogs to concentrate their efforts on the main herd.

The dangers to the herd seem to shift with the season. With the spring snowstorms no longer a threat to baby lambs, now it's West Nile virus caused by mosquitoes, various poisonous plants that are scattered here and there throughout the range, and other heat-related afflictions. Only the threat posed by predators is constant, although even that threat is lessened up in the open hillsides. A wider variety of predators will greet the herd in the river bottom once we arrive there.

One day I noticed that an adult ewe with two big lambs had dropped back from the herd, her ears drooping down the sides of her face, a sign of ill health. Although her appetite was good, when I approached, the ewe turned her head and I saw it was swollen, much the way a human's face swells with a severe allergic re-

The bum lambs readily respond to the sight of a bottle.

action. The ewe had heavily swollen eyelids and even had an extra chin where liquid had accumulated. She had bighead, an illness caused by eating a specific plant. A toxin in the plant causes sunlight sensitivity and the swelling head is the animal's allergic reaction to sunlight. I was thankful that the next few days were overcast, helping to ease her symptoms. The ewe would survive to raise her lambs, but we would mark her as a cull to be removed from our herd and ship her to market in the fall, since the disease causes permanent liver damage.

In his inventory of poisonous plants on this range, Jim has found lupine, horsebrush, locoweed, death camas, and henbane. Poison comes in many flavors on the steppe, and since there aren't any widespread infestations, we just have to take our chances with the sheep, hoping none of them gets a hankering for the taste of something lethal.

Pete had one of the herders move all his late-lambers over into my herd, since I'm willing to continue tending to ewes and his herds were on the trail, headed into the high country for the summer. His ewes are young, and are a good match for my girls. I'm thankful most of them have been going into labor in the early hours of the morning, having their lambs in the cool hours of the day. It's lambing in hot weather that I fear—cooling down a hot lamb right after its birth would mean taking it from its mother and dunking it in cold water. The nearest cold water is the river, four miles away. I know if I have to save a lamb from heat stroke, it will probably end up a bum, since it is unlikely these wild-range ewes will accept their lambs once I've washed away their birth scents, which are key to a ewe identifying her lamb. Lambs born in the cool seasons grow well and have ravenous appetites, but those born in hot temperatures can be lethargic, spending little time eating.

It's time to move my camp again, and I debate about which hill to inhabit next. It's evident that shepherds are just as predictable as their herds, because every hill I select for my camp we later discover was once a camp to a herder in the past. From rusty Prince Albert cans to old knives and heavy glass bottles, the landscape is littered with relics from those who trod this range before.

With the major effort of lambing behind us, my constant presence isn't necessary, and I start to sleep at home a few nights a week, arriving back on the range at daylight. It's a wonder my journeys to the home ranch don't take even more time than they do, since I'm easily distracted by all there is to see along the way. One day in my travels back and forth to the house from the sheep, I saw a fox kit lying on a mound of dirt near the osprey nest on the hill near our house. Upon observation Jim and I learned that the mound was a fox den, inhabited by three kits and one adult. The mother fox was busy killing prairie dogs to bring back to the den, so we were able to watch the youngsters while the mother was absent.

The red fox is the most common fox native to North America. Despite its name, this species can range in color from red or black to blonde or silver, although red is most common. Fox in the Yellowstone region are reported to show high frequencies of blonde and gray coat colors, with the frequency of novel coat colors significantly increasing at higher elevations.

The range of the red fox has greatly increased in recent years, including throughout the Green River Basin. Fox are like coyotes in being food opportunists, feeding on prairie dogs, rabbits, mice, bird eggs, insects, and whatever else is available.

Red fox generally produce four to nine kits, which are weaned at about a month old and disperse in the late summer. Adults weigh up to about fifteen pounds, with males slightly heavier than females. The average life span of a fox in the wild is three to six years. Fox are crepuscular, meaning most active at dawn and dusk.

The fox den was located beneath an osprey platform erected the year before by the power company, so perhaps the mother had hoped

An osprey flies above, headed to her nesting platform.

to benefit from any stray fish dropped from above. Osprey pairs haul sticks and various building materials to power poles in an attempt to create new nests, but in the process, they knock out electrical power to residences and businesses in the region and sometimes electrocute themselves. Although owl decoys are placed on power poles to discourage raptors from nesting or perching on live wires, some ospreys remain undeterred; some even use the owl's head as a perch.

To reduce the potential for electrocuted birds and power outages, utility company crews tear down the dangerous nests and erect nesting platforms nearby so that ospreys can continue producing young in the area. The ospreys quickly adopt the new platform nesting structures, bringing material in for construction of new nests—this time in a safe place. Ospreys are attracted to areas near open water, where they catch fish, their major food source. During the nesting season, it's not unusual to see ospreys in flight with open-mouthed fish in their clutches, returning to the nest.

A real sight to see is the osprey engaged in the act of catching fish. One hot summer day back at the home ranch, I was out among the sheep when I heard a fantastic splashing coming from the New Fork River. Every few minutes, I would hear the sound again. I made my way to the river's edge and stood transfixed as an aggressive young osprey practiced his fish-catching skills. The osprey would hover in the air, flapping his wings as he scanned the water for a likely target, and then quickly drop after his prey, pulling up at the last second to plunge his feet and body into the water. After a failed try, the bird shook the excess water from his feathers and rose back into the air for another attempt. It did not succeed while I was watching, but my heart was cheering him on.

CHAPTER 9

rangeland sentinel

◇ ◇ ◇

I awakened in the morning expecting to feel achy and sore from the previous day's hard labor, but was relieved to find myself none the worse for wear. Yesterday we docked the lambs, which means shortening their tails to reduce the possibility of fecal matter accumulating on their hindquarters, which can lead to health problems. A crew of three Nepali herders and three young American men arrived at camp for this purpose and within minutes had set up a portable pen for sheep handling. The American trio consisted of Pete's son Lou and his cousin David, both twenty-one, and my nineteen-year-old Cass. These men work from dawn to dusk, traveling from herd to herd on Pete's range, docking and doing other hard manual labor, as their dirty faces, bloody shirts, and toned bodies attest. They might get one day off from the ranch a month, and all three are currently girlfriendless. Instead, they take their pleasure from hard work and genuine camaraderie. Few of their friends would understand the lives they are leading or appreciate the satisfaction it brings them.

I spent an hour slowly moving the ewes and lambs down from the hills toward where I expected the men to erect the pen while I gathered the sheep. The wind was blowing and the herd had gone up, with lambs scattered all over one steep hillside, laid out in luxurious sleep in the warm sunshine and out of the wind's reach, with a magnificent golden eagle perched above them. Soaring in on a thermal, the eagle had arrived from the back side, silently alighting on the peak of the hill completely unnoticed by the resting herd. Turning slightly, with golden wings spread wide, the bird simply dropped into the air off the

---

Overleaf: Soaring in on a thermal, the golden eagle takes my breath away.

The herd is moved into a set of portable pens for docking.

back side of the peak when I appeared. The gracefulness of the raptor's action took my breath away—silent stalker of the sky.

This was my second such encounter of the day. Earlier in the
morning when I started to gather the sheep, I had checked the back
side of the second highest hill in the area, and found a ewe with her
days-old lamb hiding there, with a golden eagle perched above. When
I arrived, the eagle, with that same slight twist to the side, dropped off
the hill and disappeared. When the wind blows, these eagles are able

to move silently, without flapping their wings, and land above other animals without attracting attention. In neither case were the eagles behaving aggressively toward the lambs, but were perched, watching all activity that went on below. By now, most of the lambs weigh from twenty to forty pounds, so it's not as though an eagle would expect to snatch one from the ground and fly off for a feast. I once again noticed the shyness of the prairie dogs in the area, and suspect that their quickness to dive for cover is the result of eagle predation.

The men came out to help corral the last of the sheep into the pen,

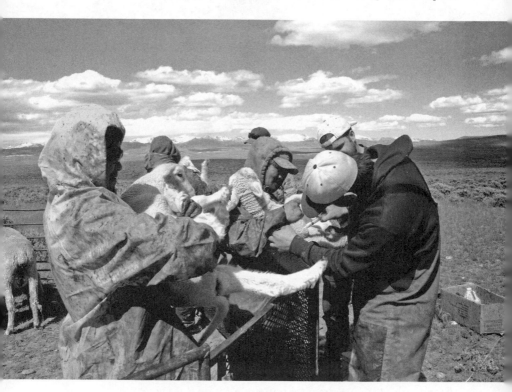

The docking crew processes the lambs.

quickly separating the herd into three smaller groups so that none of the smaller lambs would get crushed by the larger animals. Lou climbed in and grabbed all the lambs that were just a few days old, handing them to the herders outside the pen so they could be processed first. I joined the herders in handling the lambs, leading them through a processing line whereby David injected a dose of vaccine under the skin of a foreleg, and Lou applied a second vaccine by scraping the inside of a back leg, then cut off tails and, for the males, the testes, in firm, quick movements, dropping the testes into the "Rocky Mountain oyster" bucket and the tails into a pile for counting later. Cass completed the assembly-line processing, using a hot metal cauterizing rod to stop the bleeding to the tail cut and applying a powder to prevent infection.

In our years of docking and castrating lambs, we had always used a different method—that of applying rubber rings that stop blood flow, resulting in the tail and scrotum falling off within a few weeks, so this quick-and-bloody method was a first for me, although a long tradition in western ranching. While my sensibilities might have been a bit more offended by the new method, the lambs appeared to experience less discomfort and pain. Apparently the bloodless method, while seeming more humane to me, was not better for the animal it was inflicted upon.

The crew talked and laughed, and even sang and danced, as they worked, with Lou giving instruction to all, making sure the work was not just completed, but done well. The lambs were handled with care, although I was the only one actually kissing their faces as I ushered them through the processing. The crew had efficiently docked a few hundred lambs in a few hours before releasing the last of the herd and disassembling the pen. The men then swiftly loaded the pen back into the trailer and departed, headed for the last herd to finish the year's docking. I quietly walked around my herd, watching as ewes found their lambs and paired back up. All the guardian dogs were in attendance, and were rewarded with the pile of severed lamb tails. After chewing on a few, the dogs lost interest, but stayed among the resting herd, worriedly guarding over the tender lambs.

While I slept the sleep of the exhausted that night in my own bed at home, the herd remained on the grassy knoll where the docking had taken place, safe with their canine companions and burros.

Patrolling the sagebrush on the other side of the river from me, a big white pickup truck with many bright lights attached to its roll bar cruises along the two-track roads, a fully equipped law-enforcement officer at the wheel, looking for violators of public-lands regulations. He trains his binoculars on my camp and takes notes. I imagine him scrutinizing every aspect of my environs, and bristle at the inescapable feeling that I am under suspicion. I keep a clean and compact camp, and am careful to locate it at the edge of hills so as to not appear obtrusive to any other visitors to these, our public lands. These federal rangers, and the bureaucracy they represent, get under my skin. We call them "angers with an *r*" because of the us-against-them attitude they seem to embody. I know I'm probably being unfair about it; but I like to think that government representatives packing a gun are here to protect and serve, not to assume that we are all out here doing something wrong. It's symptomatic of a bigger issue: the heavy-handed, mandates-from-above form of land management used in the West.

In 2009 the Nobel Prize in economics was awarded to an Indiana professor for her work on economic governance, with an emphasis on cooperation. I yearn for Professor Elinor Ostrom's theory to be put to work in terms of natural resources and management of public lands.

Ostrom asserts that active participation of users in creating and enforcing rules is essential, and that rules that are imposed from the outside or unilaterally dictated by powerful insiders have less legitimacy and are more likely to be violated. Likewise, monitoring and enforcement work better when conducted by insiders than by outsiders. These principles are in stark contrast to the common view that monitoring and sanctioning are the responsibility of government and should be conducted by public employees.

Many natural resources, such as fish stocks, pastures, woods, lakes, and groundwater basins are managed as common property, in that various users have access to the resource in question. Ostrom notes that if we want to halt the degradation of our natural environment and prevent a repetition of the many collapses of natural-resource stocks experienced in the past, we should learn from the successes and failures of common-property regimes. Ostrom's work teaches about the deep mechanisms that sustain cooperation in human societies.

In its statement announcing the award, the Nobel Committee said this of Ostrom: "It has frequently been suggested that common ownership entails excessive resource utilization, and that it is advisable to reduce utilization either by imposing government regulations, such as taxes or quotas, or by privatizing the resource. The theoretical argument is simple: each user weighs private benefits against private costs, thereby neglecting the negative impact on others.

"However, based on numerous empirical studies of natural-resource management, Elinor Ostrom has concluded that common property is often surprisingly well managed. Thus, the standard theoretical argument against common property is overly simplistic. It neglects the fact that users themselves can both create and enforce rules that mitigate overexploitation. The standard argument also neglects the practical difficulties associated with privatization and government regulation."

Ostrom presented several case studies in the effects of cooperation, including one focused on the management of grasslands in Asia, using satellite images of Mongolia and neighboring areas in China and Russia where livestock have been feeding on large grassland areas for centuries. Historically, the region was dominated by nomads who practiced transhumance, moving herds with the seasons. In Mongolia, these traditions were largely intact in the mid-1990s, while neighboring areas in China and Russia had been exposed to radically different governance regimes, including government-imposed state-owned agricultural collectives, where most users settled permanently, with the resulting heavily degraded land in both China and Russia.

In the early 1980s, in an attempt to reverse the degradation, China dissolved the People's Communes and privatized much of the grassland of Inner Mongolia, and individual households gained ownership of specific plots of land. Again, as in the case of the collectives, this policy encouraged permanent settlement rather than pastoralism, with further land degradation as a result. As satellite images clearly revealed, both socialism and privatization are associated with worse long-term outcomes than those observed in traditional group-based governance.

A second case illustrates that user management of local resources can be more successful than management by outsiders. This case of failed modernization examined irrigation systems in Nepal, where locally managed irrigation systems have successfully allocated water between users for a long time. Most of the dams are small and primitive, built from stone, mud, and trees. The Nepalese government, with assistance from foreign donors, stepped in to build modern dams of concrete and steel. Despite flawless engineering, many of these projects have ended in failure. The reason is that the presence of durable dams has severed the ties between head-end and tail-end users. Since the dams are durable, there is little need for cooperation among users in maintaining them. Therefore, head-end users can extract a disproportionate share of the water without fearing the loss of tail-end maintenance labor. Ultimately, the total crop yield is frequently higher around the primitive dams than around the modern dams.

Ostrom's work put an international spotlight on the importance of citizen involvement in public-lands management. I hold out hope that one day her good ideas will be widely implemented.

It rained last night just before dark, washing the dust off the range and making the steppe appear heavenly serene. The sheep began moving off their bedding ground early, talking with each other as they grazed the moist morning's offerings. The herd grazed down the ridge past my camp, dropping off guardian dogs for breakfast on their way. I fed the dogs and went out to backtrack the herd, finding three of the late-lambing ewes with new lambs at their sides. They were in a nice nursery bunch on a grassy hillside not far from my camp. I decided it was time to get a count of these long-tailed lambs, so I slowly drove the truck through the sagebrush, moving along next to the herd and keeping a tally of undocked lambs as I went. Abe was in the cab with me, with Rena riding along on the flatbed, something I rarely allow because I'm afraid she'll fall off, but she loves riding on the back and I indulge her now and then. I was up to seven new lambs on my tally when I saw a group of ewes and lambs trailing up out of a draw, accompanied by a tan guardian dog with a black mask. It was Mikey, an eight-month-old pup that had been born to Vega, Rant's sister. I had raised Mikey and his two siblings for their first few months of life, bonding them with lambs in the kennel behind our house. He had left one of Pete's herds to make a jaunt over to my herd to visit. I was glad to see him, and he greeted me with enthusiasm. Rena initially wanted to attack him, but as soon as she got close to Mikey, she recognized him and they broke into a running play. What a pleasant morning— with the healthy newborn lambs, followed by a visit from Mikey, who had grown into a big and handsome young dog.

As the herd moved and the dogs played, I watched as one lamb stood up in the sagebrush and braced its legs—an odd movement for the animal. It was a muscular ewe lamb, weighing about forty pounds. As I watched, the lamb didn't move further, and its head didn't turn to watch the dogs playing nearby. Something was definitely wrong. Mikey got to the lamb before I did, approaching her quietly and licking her face, but the lamb responded by collapsing on the ground in front of him. Mikey jumped back in alarm, and the lamb's mother came running through the brush to her aid just as I arrived to assess the situation. Although lying down on her belly, the lamb was weaving unsteadily and seemed unaware of what was going on around her. I

Mikey stops by for a visit, and rests near the herd.

picked the lamb up into my arms and carried her to the truck, leaving her head and front legs in my lap so I could cuddle her close to quell her racing heartbeat and keep her calm. No fever, no frothing at the mouth, no signs of illness, no wounds or bleeding. Racing heartbeat, sensitivity to touch, condition worsening quickly. She arched her neck backwards in the death pose I knew too well, her eyes rolling back, and kicked a few times as life left her young, firm body. It was over quickly; by the time we pulled into my camp for my veterinary kit, she had died in my lap. Poisoning was doubtful, Pete reported when he answered my frantic call; tetanus was more likely. The lambs had been docked two weeks prior, and a tetanus shot given then, but protection is not immediate. Pete said he'd bet this was an isolated case, but suggested I keep a close watch on the lambs.

Of course the excitement of meeting Mikey and the business with the lamb had disrupted my long-tailed lamb tally, and I gave up on that task for the day. Now it was time to patrol and watch the herd, paying close attention for any early signs of trouble. I worried the day away. Although my early-season fears had centered on the impact of freezing blizzards, it gradually changed to the threat of predators taking their toll on newborn lambs. Now the threat—to my herd, and to my livelihood—was unknown.

Although there wasn't any more trouble with lambs that day, it returned in the form of dogs. Rant, who had been at camp all day and was unaware Mikey was guarding the herd, came out in the evening to discover the young visitor. Rant immediately went on the offensive, and Mikey took refuge under my pickup truck, enraging Rant even more and leaving me stuck, unable to move the vehicle. When Mikey did finally venture out, Rant attacked him unmercifully despite Mikey's complete submission. The only way to end the conflict was for me to unload my .22 magnum loudly over the top of the wrestling dogs, sending all the dogs running for cover. Since I'd left the door to the truck open, Rant, Rena, and Abe all jumped in the cab, with Rant and Rena snarling at each other over not having enough room. I kicked Rena and Abe back out, and I drove Rant to the camp and left him locked inside my truck. I loaded a protesting Mikey into another pickup truck and drove him toward Pete's ranch, stopping on a hill to call Cass to arrange a dog transfer. Mikey was still freaked out from the beating he'd taken from Rant, slobbering and farting as we drove, threatening to puke or do worse inside the cab of my truck, nervously chewing on the partially opened windows, and I had to keep one hand ahold of the rope I'd looped firmly through his collar as I drove the manual-transmission truck over the rough road out the back side of the pasture. Cass met me about halfway and relieved me of Mikey, returning him to the herd from which he'd been missing. Perhaps the dog would think twice the next time he contemplated leaving his herd to take a neighborhood jaunt, recalling his encounter with Rant. With Mikey safely out of the way, I set Rant free when I returned, exhausted, back to camp.

On my rounds the previous morning, the sheep were clearly spooked. I had a look around to see if I could determine the source of their agitation, but nothing seemed amiss and I continued my check of the lambs. A little later, I spotted the burros at the bottom of a nearby draw, braying and pawing the ground, churning up dirt as they fussed. On my approach, I quickly realized it was the smell of fresh blood that had the animals so alarmed. Coyotes had killed a ewe during the night. The ewe was a late-lamber that had separated off from the herd to begin labor. Her twin lambs were never able to draw a breath, and were still inside the birth sac, lying on the ground next to their mother's partially consumed carcass. I ran the burros off from the scene, but left the carcasses in place. The guardian dogs would soon find them, and wait for the coyotes to return to their feast.

My last camp move had put me atop the highest ridge in the center of the pasture, in a place we've dubbed Eagle Point. In the company of the golden eagle that perches on this rocky hillside are the bullbats—nighthawks. I often find these beautiful birds crouched on the hillside nearby, but it's only through movement that their presence is revealed, since they blend in so well to this landscape. That such a delicate-looking winged animal would bellow like a bull is a wonder of nature.

My new campsite overlooks the spring, and I can see for miles in all directions. I've been keeping a close eye on the spring, with the water level in the reservoir dropping a little every day. We've only a few days left before the hot afternoon sun takes over, causing more moisture to evaporate than the spring's daily output, and that's when we'll have to do the next big push, getting the herd to the river.

When I approached the herd in the pickup truck the next morning, they were already grazing down the hill, headed for the spring. Luv's Girl and Rant appeared from within the herd, but Luv's Girl was walking with a very visible limp—an injured front foot she didn't want me to touch. The herd slowly worked its way to the spring, with the dogs accompanying them. The dogs eventually went to my camp for food, and loitered there for the remainder of the heat of the day. Luv's Girl's foot became quite swollen, and she spent much time licking the dried mud from between her toes. By the end of the day, she was very sore, and was still insistent that I leave the wound alone.

Attentive to his mate, Rant is very concerned about Luv's Girl's foot as well, gently sniffing it, but not nudging or upsetting his girl in the process. When night began to fall, the guardians returned to the herd, Luv's Girl doggedly limping her way into the middle of the herd she must always protect. The next morning, she was doing a little better, but I offered her a ride to camp in the pickup truck and she jumped in enthusiastically. She jumped out to lick the noses of the bum lambs, drank some water, and then fell asleep in the brush next to camp. Rant arrived at camp, and was soon sleeping by her side.

Two days after the discovery of the dead ewe, Jim and I decided to return to the draw to check on the carcass. When we approached, we flushed a small group of ravens and magpies from the nearly completely consumed ewe. The birthing sac with the lambs was gone as well. Scattered pieces of bone and wool were all that remained, and the vegetative matter that had spilled onto the ground from the ewe's torn rumen. I walked around in the soft dirt and sand in the draw, looking at the tracks and traces of all the animals that had visited the scene. The chewed bones were the work of coyotes, and the wool the work of an eagle as it tore chunks of meat from the carcass. Here and there were feathers and tracks of smaller birds like the magpies and ravens. I walked slowly, trying to read the story the dirt told, finding several sets of coyote tracks. Jim followed the imprints left by one coyote as it walked away from the carcass, headed up the narrow draw. He turned a corner of the draw and lost the trail due to the grass growth, but a fluttering from the hillside above caught his attention. We hiked up out of the draw to find the carcass of a coyote, blonde-colored fur gently waving in the afternoon breeze. The coyote had a bloody head and deep puncture wounds at its throat, but was otherwise intact. Jim nudged the carcass with his boot to show that although its body was stiff with rigor mortis, no other predator had touched it. Luv's Girl had won this battle, though it had been fierce, resulting in the wound to her foot. I can imagine the coyote on his back in battle with the big dog, managing to bite her front foot before she crushed his throat in her jaws, ending his life as the coyote had ended the life of the pregnant ewe.

We awoke to an overcast morning. It was the weekend, and Jim had spent the night in camp so we could be up early to move the herd before it became too hot. The warm July temperatures had exhausted the spring; the earthen reservoir was nearly dry. What was once a wa-

The herd rests high in the hills before the big push to the river.

tery oasis had become a dangerous draw of black muck. The small amount of standing water on the surface served as a temptation for the sheep, and they would wade into the muck only to become stuck. It was time to move to a new water source. It was time for the big push to the river.

We began with the sheep still high in the hills on their bed-grounds. Since we often walk among the herd to check their welfare, our mere presence isn't enough to move the herd. We communicate our intentions by clapping our hands a few times and calling out "Hup! hup!" while Abe goes into chivvy mode, pacing back and forth at the edge of the herd. This time the sheep moved out quickly, headed downhill toward the depleted spring. We let them water under our watchful eyes, then began the push again, getting them to follow the ridge swales on a continued downhill route. This is the time that Abe is happiest, when he can work next to his human partners in moving the sheep. He knows what needs to be done and does it, without anyone issuing commands. By the time we dropped the herd over the last hill and into the green river bottom a few hours later, we had traveled five miles, with the herd browsing on fresh rangelands all the way. A few ewes with new lambs dropped back from the herd along the way, and we allowed them to stay behind, not wanting to stress the new babes. They would rejoin the herd later, when the lambs were a few hours older.

The herd lined the riverside, taking long drinks of the fresh cold water in the Big Sandy River before bedding down in the grass nearby. They spent the heat of the day there, moving back up into the safety of

Overleaf: Sheep line the riverbank to quench their thirst.

the highlands before darkness fell again, their livestock guardian dogs their constant companions.

Three researchers with the University of California at Berkeley (Lucy Diekmann, Lee Panich, and Chuck Striplen), in a 2007 article for *Rangelands,* the journal of the Society for Range Management, critiqued the widespread notion that the American landscape before European contact was unworked. The millions of Native Americans living in every part of this continent prior to the arrival of Europeans managed and manipulated ecosystems in a manner that produced needed commodities—from food and medicine to raw materials and ceremonial regalia. An intense knowledge of species and ecosystems, and how these resources responded to different management regimes, was required. Discounting the influence of Native American management was once an excuse for ignoring Native rights and claims, curtailment of their traditional management practices, and in some cases justified removal from their traditional lands so that "pristine" landscapes could be created, especially in national parks. The researchers suggest it would be more accurate and helpful to think of precolonial landscapes not as untouched wilderness but "as cultured landscapes, and perhaps working landscapes, in which human use also has the potential to enhance ecosystem productivity and diversity."

One hot dry afternoon, as I drove down a two-track road in the sheep pasture, I came upon two golden eagles on the ground. The raptors rose heavily into the air, weighed down by a recent meal. I drove straight to the spot in the sagebrush where the eagles had been grounded, and discovered the fresh remains of a pronghorn antelope fawn. This predation event was about three and a half miles from the one I had witnessed a few weeks earlier. That earlier event also involved two golden eagles, and I've every reason to assume it was the same two. I photographed the eagles and the remains of the fawns in both events. If these two eagles are keying on pronghorn fawns, imagine the success they could have in this vast sagebrush steppe.

I wondered once again about the impact of eagle predation on fawns in areas with abundant eagle populations. Sheep producers in eastern Wyoming have told us that golden eagles sometimes take a hard toll on their lamb crops, until pronghorn fawning begins and the eagles switch to fawns. I see golden eagles frequently in the sheep pasture, even perched on hillsides above the sheep, but I am thankful to report we haven't had any problems with them. I think the fact that our guardian dogs don't like big birds has something to do with it.

Later in the month I had another interesting pronghorn encounter. The pronghorn antelope fawns were growing well, but their long legs looked out of proportion with their young bodies at this stage of growth. Three times one week I watched pronghorns jumping over a woven-wire fence, something that supposedly happens only rarely since pronghorn prefer to go under fences. The first time Jim and I witnessed this, we were driving near a neighbor's fence when I noticed a line of pronghorn trailing along the far side of the fence. When the group approached a low spot in the woven wire, the first doe jumped the fence and cleared it. I realized the rest of the herd might follow, so I stopped to watch as the next two does took their turns, easily clearing the wire. The fawns did not follow, and at that point, our presence was noticed and the animals hurried away from the fence-line.

A week later, I saw a pronghorn doe and her two fawns near the same fence again, and watched as the doe jumped over the fence in the same spot. I was running late, and didn't have time to stop and watch the behavior of the rest of the herd.

The next morning, I went back by the fence again, and this time saw one doe with three fawns. By the time I arrived, one fawn was on my side of the fence, with the remainder of the group on the far side. Hoping not to disturb them, I parked the truck at some distance from the group and sat and watched. After a few minutes of staring in my direction, the doe finally moved forward, jumping the fence. She patiently waited as the other two fawns nervously milled and finally jumped single-file over the fence to join her and the third fawn as they moved away. This was an excellent lesson in learned behavior, and gives me hope for the ability of this species to adapt to human changes in its environment.

By midsummer I had developed a close personal relationship with two broods of sage grouse, and Jim told me I needed to end it soon. I knew he was right, but I hated to have to break ties with them nonetheless.

The two broods—one with five youngsters, the other with six—range close together. I had first observed them at dawn and then dusk on a section of state ground near an old loading pen, and a few weeks ago I started seeking them out. Of course they were initially alarmed when I pulled up in my noisy truck. But I stayed in the vehicle, photographing them through the driver's side window and talking to them in soothing tones, and they soon calmed. I was gradually able to get out of the truck and walk around them, and to sit on the ground in front of them. I continued to talk to them, and they replied in grouse song. What floored me was how similar these grouse were to the domestic chickens my family had raised on our farm when I was a child. They act and vocalize just like chickens. As a child, I had a favorite hen named Half N Half (she was half white, half red) who used to accompany me on short walks and would sit on my lap while I read aloud to her. Yes, I was reading to a chicken long before reading to therapy animals came into vogue.

My experience with the two sage grouse broods took me back to my childhood. I was tickled when the adolescent grouse walked up beside me to check out the yellow thread hemming my pant leg, and when they tilted their heads to the side to watch hawks fly overhead, and sang as they took dust baths, and preened their feathers, using a tuft of sagebrush to break the wind. The two hens were far more cautious, remaining about twenty feet away, strolling slowly around the edge of their broods, calling to them and keeping an eye on me.

I hadn't tried to tame these birds; I hadn't fed them. I'd just been near them in a nonthreatening way, and apparently that was enough to gain acceptance. I'd had an extraordinary time getting to know them, but I also knew my place, and theirs. I finally had to force myself to go by them without stopping. They don't need to know me, but it had been a pleasure to get to know them just a little, for just a short time.

◇ ◇ ◇ ◇

Although degradation of dryland ecosystems is often blamed on over-grazing by livestock and mismanagement by pastoralists, that assumption is being challenged. As a 2008 report by the World Initiative for Sustainable Pastoralism noted, "degradation has instead been attributed to a combination of constraints to pastoralism, through restrictions of mobility and privatization of land, and substitution of pastoralism with less sustainable forms of livestock keeping. Research has shown that where mobility and locally owned institutions for land management are maintained, the results can be biodiversity conservation and sustainable land management."

While China works under the assumption that pastoralism is harmful to the steppe environment, and has adopted policy goals of sedentarizing pastoralists and transforming pastoralism, other countries have challenged such thinking, instead focusing their actions on adopting policies that bridge problems of continued pastoralism, allowing pastoralism to be used as a tool for reversing land degradation.

The report explained: "Many of the world's drylands are considered to be co-evolved with large herds of herbivorous animals, to the extent that they are to some extent grazing-dependent. Livestock may have replaced wild herbivores in these systems, but many drylands display a degree of dependence on livestock grazing, and those environments have been further modified through the land management practices of pastoralists in recent centuries. Conservation therefore may depend on the effective continuation of pastoralism, and it is clear that both cessation and restriction of pastoralism lead to environmental degradation."

The report addressed various criticisms of pastoralism, economic, environmental, and sociopolitical, and noted: "There are those who argue that mobile pastoralists follow irrational economic practices, such as hoarding of livestock or refusal to engage in a market economy. Others argue that pastoralism is inherently destructive to the environment and causes desertification because of the 'tragedy of the commons.' Elsewhere, governments consider mobility to be anarchic and pastoralists to be ungovernable, and 'not yet settled.' The outcome of these misconceptions is that alternatives to pastoralism, mostly based on privatization of land, sedentarization of people and efforts to intensify the extensive production, have been promoted at the expense of pastoralism, and to the detriment of pastoralist environments.

"These prejudices have been refuted over the past 20 years and a new understanding is emerging: of pastoralists as economically rational land-users, and of pastoralism as a successful adaptation to the high uncertainty of dryland environments."

The report concluded, "Strong arguments have been put forward for mobile livestock keeping as both a necessary adaptation that enables people to construct livelihoods in many climatically challenging environments, and as an integral component of many rangeland ecosystems, to the extent that its removal leads to loss of ecosystem health and resilience."

The sheep herd spends the tranquil days of summer gravitating from one hillside and draw to the next, moving down to water for frequent sating drinks, and resting during the heat of the day. The lambs have long outgrown their tiny long-legged bodies, and are now rippling with muscle and fat, their bodies chubby and rounded from eating

Rena enjoys a breeze after taking a swim in the river.

lush vegetation and drinking their mother's milk. They pant open-mouthed from the heat. The dogs come to camp seeking food and shade during the heat of the day, leaving the herd in the safekeeping of the burros, but returning for the night shift.

Late summer brings scalding days with temperatures reaching eighty degrees, and hazy skies resulting from forest fires near and far. Afternoon rains are both a curse and a blessing. Good for the ground, as there is rarely enough moisture in this arid landscape. But the storms produce more lightning than anything else, causing new fires to spark daily. Wildfire crews stay busy putting out new starts every day, besides battling huge, out-of-control fires throughout the West.

Shimmering heat waves over the landscape are disturbed by shadows cast by the huge wings of birds soaring above. Thirty years ago when I reported I had just seen two vultures in Sublette County, I was met with disbelief. Although still not common here, we do have a few turkey vultures in the summer these days. Our western migrants spend winters in Central or South America. Official maps of turkey vulture summer distribution indicate we still have only a few in this region of western Wyoming. They are wary of human presence and are easily disturbed here, but I know that isn't the case in areas where they are more abundant.

There are about two million turkey vultures in North America, including the small population that summers here in the Green River Basin. Although populations increased in the western United States in the mid-1980s, declines have occurred since the onset of the regional drought in the 1990s.

Deriving its name from its resemblance to the wild turkey, with its featherless red head, the turkey vulture is the most widely distributed vulture in the New World. With a highly developed sense of smell, vultures fly overhead, searching out the scent of gas produced by the beginnings of decay in dead animals. Turkey vultures benefit from human activities such as livestock production, and also from higher road densities that provide carrion in the form of roadkill.

An adult vulture has a six-foot wingspan, weighs about three

Turkey vultures move into this region during the hot summer months.

pounds, and holds its wings up in the vulture's characteristic V-shaped flight. Immature vultures have gray heads with black beak tips.

Neither the sheep nor their guardians take notice of the vultures soaring high above, and we've never encountered one on the ground near the herd, but as I walk among the sheep, watching the seemingly effortless flights above, I wonder what such an encounter would be like. These birds are wary of humans, so I will probably never know.

As I walk, my eye is drawn to a pair of young ewes. Petey was born late last year at the home ranch, the last of that season's lambs to be born. All the other lambs were older and bigger, and the small babe struggled to stay caught up with the herd—but she did. When she was about two months old, a bear entered the pasture where the herd was grazing and killed Petey's mother. Petey was then an orphan, but she still managed to stay caught up with the rest of the herd as it moved and grazed during the day. She was smart enough to position herself with other sheep around her, so she would never be caught out alone. Since she wasn't drinking her mother's rich milk, Petey was skinny, but still, she was strong.

The sheep herd was moved out of the pasture where the bear predation had occurred, and had spread out to graze along a meadow. Petey let her guard down just long enough that she was caught out alone and attacked by a fox. Petey must have struggled, because she escaped with a mangled ear and bites on her front and back legs. By the time we found her, she was very weak.

Since her injuries would prevent her from keeping up with the herd, we brought Petey to the house, installing her in the front yard on Thanksgiving morning. She was despondent but hungry, and soon took to eating the weeds and grass in an unkept corner of our yard. We filled up a water bucket and an oat bucket, and went back to the herd to retrieve a companion lamb for her. Friendly's daughter Pea soon joined Petey in the yard, along with a bale of hay. Within a few hours, Petey had perked up.

Little Petey had the will to live. When I look out onto the herd grazing the sagebrush steppe, the sight of these two beautiful and fit yearling ewes, Petey and Pea, strolling together, gives me such pleasure. Looking at her today, no one would have reason to suspect that Petey had been through such hard times, orphaned by a bear, attacked by a fox, but thriving today.

My fellow sheep producers summer their herds in the mountains that surround this valley, up in the wilderness where there is no vehicle access, or in high-elevation areas where there are large predators as well as human recreationists, many who have never personally met a sheep or their guardian dogs and are not prepared for such encounters. Some hikers are alarmed and disturbed when they encounter large barking dogs on the edge of a sheep herd, and later demand that the public range be rid of these animals. That makes me sad, because I feel that if they only understood and appreciated what they encountered on the range, the ecological benefits of the grazing system, they would treasure it as I do. Conservationists must work to bring that understanding to the nation, before this important and valuable way of life is lost.

Bulgaria uses transhumance grazing in the highlands to maintain mountain meadows for the conservation of species that prefer open ares. The imperial eagle, lesser kestrel, and Saker falcon are all highly dependent on the existence of open, well-grazed habitats. Since restoring a transhumance program in the Kotel Mountain area, Bulgarian officials have documented the return of three species of birds to the region: lesser grey shrike, woodchat shrike, and the long-legged buzzard. These steppe-dwelling species are now breeding in the region for the first time in more than fifty years.

The days and weeks pass, and I'm stunned to realize it's August. I've weaned the bum lambs from the milk bucket and turned their attention to whole oats I feed once a day. Soon the bums will abandon my camp and become part of the larger herd. I'm weaning myself off the sheep camp and the range as well, sleeping at home at night, driving out to check on the animals during the day. They no longer need my constant attention, and it's both a relief and a letdown. I will miss living and breathing alongside them.

Driving around the pasture one evening, Jim and I looked up on a ridge to see a large golden eagle perched in the middle of the sheep herd. The scene nearly made my heart stop. I reasoned with myself to be calm, but it took an effort. It's one thing to observe an eagle hunting adjacent to the sheep—it's another thing entirely to find that eagle amid the herd. The sun was setting, and the sheep had been grazing across a high ridge, headed to its bedding ground. Our sentinel golden eagle sat serenely in one spot, as the herd grazed close in and around it. When we flushed the eagle, it took to a nearby hillside, where another smaller eagle was also perched. The eagles stayed nearby as the sheep grazed.

Our ewes weigh about two hundred pounds, and our resident eagle looked enormous as it sat atop the sagebrush among them, yet we know it probably weighs only about ten pounds. A coyote pup approaching this herd would make a quick and easy meal for the raptor. But something tells me it is no threat to my lambs. Only time will tell if I have made a grave error in judgment.

By mid-month, scalding afternoons fade into late-day thunderstorms, and overnight temperatures plunge into the thirties, as if fall were already here. The spring that had sustained the herd for so long is now a tiny puddle, frequented on occasion by a few pronghorn and ravens. A blind has been set up inside the earthen reservoir, a sign that bowhunters will arrive soon, followed by riflemen within a month, as grazing gives way to hunting on this shared landscape. By then, it will be time for us to go—to ship the lambs, and load the trucks for home. I'll surely miss this country, this sagebrush sea that engulfs my soul.

What had started as a simple—if stunning—observation was now a common occurrence. In my checks of the sheep herd I often flush our golden eagle from the top of the hill above them. Not every day, but nearly every day. It happens in the morning, afternoon, and evening— whatever time of day I approach the herd. The guardian dogs became accustomed to the eagle, and didn't erupt in alarm when the bird took flight. Lambing was long past, and the eagle did not seem to pose a threat to the herd.

Having moved from my camp back to my house and driving out to check the sheep every day, I soon began to look for the eagle as I searched out the herd. I would drive along a ridge, coming up on the eagle from behind, and by its presence I would know that my herd was grazing down below.

It soon became evident that as the herd moved, the eagle moved with them, flying out in front, so it was always ahead of the sheep. I sat on the hillside one afternoon as the herd moved down a long draw in front of me, and watched the eagle fly back and forth, perched on one side of the draw, then flying farther down the draw to perch on the opposite side, watching the herd as it moved. That's when it dawned on me: the golden eagle was using the herd's movement in hunting for its next meal. One of the guardian dogs uses a similar hunting technique.

Luv's Girl often hunts jackrabbits. When the herd is on the move, she walks along with the front line of sheep. She has learned from experience that the movement of the herd displaces the jacks, whereupon she can run down and kill the hares flushed from their hiding places.

I'm not positive that I'm right about what the golden was doing, because I haven't actually seen it take a jackrabbit from near the herd. But I'll keep watching, hoping I get to witness a successful hunt, and that my presence isn't too much of a disruption.

My friend Mark Churchill, a Nebraska falconer, tells me that observations like mine are what led to the creation of falconry. Some herder, thousands of years ago, watched an eagle as it hunted and took action to join that hunt, becoming the first falconer. Mark called this herder his "ancestor of the heart." I love the vision and feeling this brings to mind, a Kazakh herder, so long ago, and a world away, seeing things and interpreting them in the same way as I do today.

Watching a golden eagle live in such close association with the sheep herd has been an interesting experience for this shepherd. At another time of year, and perhaps under different circumstances or a different place, I might dread the presence of a golden eagle nearby because of the threat it could pose to my herd, and to my livelihood. But not this time, at this place, under these circumstances. Instead, our golden has become something of a welcome presence, a rangeland sentinel.

leaving the range

◇ ◇ ◇ ◇

Opening day of bowhunting season for pronghorn antelope fell on a Sunday in mid-August, and brought with it a surprising change. The addition of just a few more people, with a little more traffic sailing forth on the sagebrush sea, resulted in an abrupt alteration in pronghorn behavior. The size of the groups of pronghorn in the area had been increasing little by little throughout the summer, and for the most part the animals regarded me and my ranch truck as just another part of the scenery. Within just a few days of the arrival of hunting season, however, these groups would erupt in panic and run flat out to get away from my vehicle, which they had encountered on a daily basis for weeks with barely a sniff of interest. I had thought that things would remain relatively calm until rifle season opened, but evidently I'd been wrong. When I dropped into a draw one morning, a pronghorn doe took a sudden blind, running leap off an embankment to flee from the perceived threat I represented. Change had come to the range. Our time to leave was approaching.

Mornings were now frosty, and the nip in the air required sweatshirts and jackets. A full moon meant beautiful sunsets, but it also meant predators prowled throughout the night. One of my bum lambs was killed right below my camp in the hours just before sunrise. The sheep had split off into three different groups, and the bum had been caught out alone. The guardians worked overtime in moonlight, but had difficulty keeping up when the sheep were so dispersed. Jim and I walked for miles, trying to pull the sheep back into one group. We threw the bums into the pickup truck and dropped them into the big herd—no more hanging out around camp. All our hard

Overleaf: A mule deer buck pauses in the snow-covered sagebrush.

work and tender care to raise these healthy, beautiful babes, could come to naught at the jaws of a coyote. At least Paula and Dimmy were okay.

On cold fall mornings, cowbirds can often be found on the backs of the sheep, their feet firmly planted in warm wool. Cowbirds spend most of their time foraging on the ground for seed, most often at the feet of grazing animals. Originally a bison-following bird of the Great Plains, cowbirds eventually expanded their range eastward in the 1800s as forests were cleared.

Cowbirds are parasitic birds, laying their eggs in the nests of a wide range of other species, tricking the host species into hatching and raising the cowbirds' babies. I am fascinated by the fact that they

A cowbird sits on the back of a ewe.

never raise their own young. A female cowbird may lay about forty eggs per year for two years, but only 3 percent survive to adulthood. Cowbirds continuously monitor the nests they parasitize, and destroy any nests of host birds that won't care for their young. For such small things, they certainly are conniving.

My old ewe Friendly, long the leader of my sheep, had been trailing behind the herd for weeks, and late one fall afternoon as our time on the range was drawing to a close, I knew the inevitable had arrived: Friendly failed to rise from her afternoon bed. The guardian dogs had stayed with her, keeping her company while they waited for me to find them. The poor old dear was tired, and she was ready to leave us. I petted Friendly's nose and propped her into a comfortable position before seeking Jim's help in putting her down.

Jim and I both shed tears as we reflected on Friendly's life with us—at fourteen and a half years old, she'd shared over half of our twenty-five years of married life. She was one of my original sheep; looking into those beautiful dark eyes as I fed the tiny orphan lamb from a bottle is what got me hooked on raising sheep. Friendly was the smallest of the orphan lambs I purchased that year, and she quickly figured out that I kept the milk bottles in the fridge just inside the back door. When she would get hungry, she'd strike the door with her tiny front hooves, and if the door opened just a crack, she'd stick her nose in and race up the back steps to demand her milk. She had a startlingly deep voice, a hallmark sound that we've heard every day throughout the life we shared together.

We raised fifteen orphan lambs that first year. Six months in, one snowy January day, the Great Pyrenees guardian dog they lived with took them under our back fence and out for an adventure. They escaped onto the Pinedale Mesa, a big-game winter range adjacent to our ranch; an area closed to human presence in winter and that also serves as a coyote refuge. Desperate to find them before the coyotes did, Jim chartered an airplane to fly the mesa, but failed to spot them in the many folds and canyons of that rough sagebrush landscape. Finally, a week after their adventure began, they arrived at a cattle ranch seven miles away on the far side of the mesa, happily munching hay in the ranch yard. Not one had been killed or wounded, and the guardian dog was still watching over them. Friendly happily jumped into the stock trailer when Jim arrived to retrieve them.

Friendly became my herd's guide, leading the way out to new grazing in the daytime and to bedding grounds at night. When we moved the sheep, she was always first. Getting the herd to journey through dangerous places, such as across a wooden stock bridge over the New Fork River, was only possible if the lead sheep was willing to go. As long as I had ginger snaps, crackers, or granola bars in my jacket pockets, Friendly would get that herd anywhere we needed it to be.

Friendly produced lambs every year throughout her adult life—two years prior, she had triplets, and this, her final year, only a single ewe lamb.

Every day for more than a decade when I checked the sheep, I would call them and Friendly always answered in that distinctive voice of hers. She would run to me, looking for treats and a pet, sniffing my mouth to learn if I'd been snacking on something interesting.

I'd sniff her nose in return, and was often rewarded with the sweet smell of something delicious she'd been eating—rosehips, or wild-flower petals, or sagebrush buds.

Friendly was remarkable, and our family's life was blessed by our time with her gentle animal soul.

Each September morning brings a chill on the breeze, with overcast skies and the increased feeling of change. A quick storm put a layer of snow on the mountains above us, and covered our range with small white balls of hail. We are greeted each day to a thick frost blanketing the landscape, an unquestionable reminder that fall has in fact arrived on the range. Hunting blinds seem to be springing up every few miles.

When we leave the pasture, the riverside will fill up with campers and four-wheelers—pronghorn antelope hunters going after their quarry with bow or rifle. The quiet rangeland will be given over once again, to a different type of user, who may or may not love this land-scape as I do. Noisy gunshots will ring out across the range, laughter and smoke will rise from friendly campfires, and steamy gut piles of harvested animals will be consumed by hungry coyotes.

Then the snows will come, pushing out the last of the human visitors once more, laying down a white carpet to cushion the steps of the next inhabitants of the sagebrush steppe—wintering mule deer. The longest recorded migration on record for mule deer in North America is for members of the Sublette mule deer herd, which inhabit this basin.

Members of the Sublette mule deer herd seasonally migrate sixty to one hundred miles from winter range near Pinedale to summer in five different mountain ranges: Salt River Range, Wyoming Range, Wind River Range, Gros Ventre Range, and Snake River Range. By late fall, most mule deer converge to winter in one of two major complexes: the mesa, which abuts the back boundary of our home ranch, and the Pinedale Front of the Wind Rivers. Research indicates that more than thirty-five hundred deer move through a narrow bottleneck between the outlet of Fremont Lake and the town of Pinedale in seasonal migrations.

Seasonal ranges of the thirty-two-thousand-head Sublette mule deer include high-elevation summer range, mid-elevation transition range, winter range, and severe-winter relief range. Winter severity rarely becomes extreme enough to force deer from winter ranges to severe-winter relief ranges—we call it the last place they go before they die. Wyoming has only had two or three severe winters (1983–1984 and 1992–1993) in the last thirty years.

As the deer move to lower elevations in winter, so do the mountain lions that prey on them. The range of the mountain lion has historically been the largest of any land mammal in the Western Hemisphere, with the exception of humans; mountain lions now range from the southern tip of South America to northern Canada.

Rarely observed by humans, the mountain lion is a common mammal in the basin, although population counts are more like educated guesses. Lion populations throughout the West increased in abundance and distribution in the last few decades after the banning of the widespread use of poisons for predator control. According to the Wyoming Game and Fish Department, lions currently occupy most timbered and tall-shrub-covered regions statewide.

Dispersal patterns and genetic evidence suggest mountain lion populations throughout most of the western United States are well connected, due in large part to the long-range movements of male mountain lions and the relative seamlessness of the mountain range in the Rocky Mountain West. The broad geographic distribution of the mountain lion in North America attests to its ability to adapt to a variety of landscapes as long as there is adequate prey and cover.

Mountain lions are generally solitary carnivores. Dominant males typically breed with females that reside within their home range. Resident males aggressively defend their territories against male intruders, whereas females allow more overlap, but tend to avoid each other as much as possible. Females typically produce their first litter of two to four kittens by the time they are three years old (with a gestation lasting about ninety days) and may breed at any time of the year, but most are born between May and October. Kittens are weaned when they are about three months old, but they typically remain with the female for about a year and a half before becoming independent.

Our livestock guardian dogs seem to be a good deterrent against lion depredation. Lions like to sneak in covertly, making their kills under the cover of darkness. The noisy deep booms of several guardian dogs around a sheep herd makes this a rather undesirable prey source for lions, although any sheep that stray from the flock without a guardian could be easy prey. One summer when I was new to the sheep business, a lion crept down the ditch bank into my orphan

---

Overleaf: The changing of the season signifies
it's time to depart the sagebrush sea.

Mountain lions are common throughout the western range,
but rarely seen by humans.

lamb herd. The big cat carried away one fat lamb as a feast, and then ran up and down through the small herd, swatting lambs, leaving eleven dead babes in its wake.

Many of the pronghorn hunters will go from their pursuit of this open-range ungulate to the mountains for bigger game: Rocky Mountain elk. With the cooling temperatures and first snows of the season, bull elk enter breeding season or "rut," and their bugles can be heard for long distances on crisp fall mornings and evenings.

Rocky Mountain elk breeding season means the mountains are alive with bugles, squeals, and grunts. During the fall rut, bull elk spend time wallowing, thrashing trees and brush with antlers, and bugling. Increased male hormone levels causes bulls to have swollen necks, and they become busy with dominance displays with other bulls, sometimes resulting in sparring and fighting. Bulls eat little during breeding season, spending their energy on gathering cows and protecting their harems from other bulls. All this activity causes bulls to lose weight, with a loss of 100 to 150 pounds during rut not uncommon.

It's been more than a decade since the US Fish and Wildlife Service transplanted Canadian wolves into Yellowstone National Park and Central Idaho. Now there's certainly no shortage of wolves, as the wolf population has expanded hundreds of miles from its original release site. The Wyoming Game and Fish Department maintains that wolves are causing significant declines in numerous elk and moose herds in western Wyoming, depressing the number of calves to the point that the herds can't sustain themselves. Six of eight elk herds containing resident wolf packs experienced significant declines after wolves were reintroduced to the region in 1995. State wildlife managers seek to have healthy elk herds, with a calf to cow ratio of at least twenty-five calves per one hundred elk cows, but this ratio has declined in eight wolf-occupied elk herd areas since wolves took up occupancy. Some winters, gray wolves enter the feed grounds and kill and harass the elk, posing a whole new problem for wildlife managers.

The towns and campgrounds around Sublette County become filled with camouflaged-clad men with four-wheel drive trucks and hunter-orange vests and hats during elk-hunting season, providing a boon to the local economy. I'll be glad to remove my animals from this quiet range before all of that activity begins.

One fall after Pete's herds had left their mountain pastures, and the lambs had been sorted and shipped, the ewe herds began the trail south. One of the herds had just passed the town of Farson and was near the well-known landmark of Boar's Tusk, a volcanic core rising from the desert floor, when a strange ram entered the herd and began knocking the ewes end-over-end in his breeding enthusiasm. It was several months early for a ram to be in the herd, but the even bigger problem was that this was no domestic ram. It was a wild Rocky Mountain bighorn sheep, miles from his mountain habitat, but plenty pleased to encounter a bunch of females. The ram ended up having encounters with domestic ewe flocks belonging to several local sheepmen, and five months later, hybrid lambs were born to these ewes. Some of the lambs had hair instead of wool, and color markings like bighorns instead of their all-white woolly mothers.

There was a big to-do over the whole thing, and wildlife-agency folks were not on their best behavior. The problem was that state law prohibits the ownership of native wildlife and wildlife crosses. Since the incident was no fault of the sheepmen, there shouldn't have been much of an issue, but there was. The other problem is that while wildlife officials were maintaining that bighorn sheep and domestic sheep should be kept far from each other because of the disease threat posed by domestics to wild sheep, the Boar's Tusk ram's energetic foray demonstrated the fallacy of such a policy.

In the end, most of the lambs died anyway, some while in the hands of state officials. But two ranches ended up with several of the hybrid lambs. One of the lambs was born on the Erramouspe ranch in Sublette County; this little ram, named Rocky, was kept as a breeding ram. Rocky had his own set of ewes to care for and lived on the ranch for nearly a decade. I visited Rocky several times over the years, and enjoyed watching the late John Erramouspe walk out in the sage-brush to greet the big ram with a bag of oats. Rocky was impossible to keep in a corral or fence—he could breach any obstacle.

There are about seven thousand bighorn sheep in Wyoming, not including those at Yellowstone National Park. Age and size, including horn size, determine a ram's dominance. The growth rings on a ram's horn can be counted to estimate the animal's age.

Just northeast of this basin is the Whiskey Mountain bighorn win-ter range. Once the largest concentration of bighorn sheep in North America, the Whiskey Mountain herd has since declined to only a fraction of its former number. With a population once numbering nearly fifteen hundred, the herd is now less than half that size. After its population peaked, as did its forage-utilization rates on winter range, the herd experienced a pneumonia outbreak in 1991, which resulted in a population crash. Since that time, not enough lambs have sur-vived to increase the population. Although a mineral deficiency was suspected, mineral supplementation and other conservation meas-ures haven't resulted in increased lamb survival or substantial popula-tion growth. An effort to control coyotes has had positive effects, but complete recovery of this herd simply hasn't happened. Mountain lion depredation also appears to be an issue.

This basin wouldn't be the wild place that it is without two large and resilient bird species: the great blue heron and the bald eagle. Both birds remain in the area long after others have migrated out for the cold season, and they concentrate around warm springs and other open water.

The great blue heron is the largest and the most widely distributed wading bird in North America, breeding throughout the United States and wintering as far north as New England and southern Alaska. The nationwide population is estimated at eighty-three thousand. Herons are found along calm waters, and usually nest in tree colonies near water, where hundreds of birds gather. Great blue herons are thirty-eight to fifty-four inches tall, with wingspans that can be more than six feet wide.

Herons forage by walking slowly through or standing motionless

A great blue heron stands like a statue on a post.

in water and striking at prey. Although the great blue heron eats primarily fish, it is adaptable and willing to eat other animals as well.
Several studies have found that voles (small, mouse-like rodents)
were a very important part of a heron's diet, making up nearly half of
what was fed to their nestlings.

Eagles inhabit the Upper Green River Basin throughout the year,
but during winter, population dynamics change. Both bald and
golden eagles are present, but many of these birds of prey migrate
into the basin for the winter. Although bald eagles are often associ-

Both bald eagles and golden eagles inhabit the Green River Basin.

ated with open water, they spend a large portion of winter in more in-land habitat, hunting small prey and scavenging on dead livestock and wildlife. In one Yellowstone National Park study, 93 percent of ea-gles fed largely on large-animal carrion during the winter.

As winter arrives on more northerly breeding sites and lakes and rivers begin to freeze, bald eagles migrate south, with thousands mov-ing from central Canada into the United States from November through March.

The United States now has the largest population of breeding bald eagles since World War II. Bald eagles in the Lower 48 have climbed from an all-time low of 417 nesting pairs in 1963 to an estimated new high of 9,789 breeding pairs in 2007. Americans can now see wild bald eagles in every state in the Lower 48.

Eagles are fairly long-lived in captivity (up to about fifty years) but probably survive no longer than thirty years in the wild. Bald eagles develop pair bonds and usually mate for life.

As I prepared to leave the range with the herd, I took a mental tally of the season. Lambing had gone well, and our losses had been minimal. We did have more orphan lambs than I would have liked, but those that had survived were doing fine and had already been incorporated into the herd. We had lost a few sheep to predators, as well as a few to other causes, but all totaled, it hadn't been a bad year. The lambs were gaining nicely, the ewes were regaining their pre-pregnancy shapes, and lamb prices were holding. Everything was aligning to provide a modest profit this year, and the sale of the lambs would more than pay for winter feed for the ewe herd.

But events were soon to prove that my assessment had been premature. One Friday morning, my early sheep check led me to a slain ninety-pound lamb; the predator seemed to have eaten only the liver. The scene was so fresh, the kill must have just occurred—blood everywhere, upset dogs. Rant took Luv's Girl to the ground for coming near the carcass, which he was guarding but wouldn't touch. I wasn't sure how much the dogs had witnessed, if anything, but the situation was very tense.

The next day, I found a completely consumed lamb along the river—just fresh blood and the soft, peeled-back pelt remained. I notified our Wildlife Services specialists, who were responding to major wolf problems at the time. I learned that one outfit had thirty-seven sheep and one yearling steer killed, and a guardian dog had been injured. A pack of six wolves were killed by agents in an effort to stop the depredations. The next day, a pack of five wolves was killed after killing three guardian dogs and forty-five sheep.

When I learn of these events, I'm always reminded it could easily be our ranch and our animals. While this time it's three guardian dogs belonging to someone else, it could just as easily have been our dear guardians. Our losses were much smaller in comparison to the kills experienced by our fellow producers, but we were all at risk. Our sheep were spooked, the dogs were on edge, and things were in a general state of unrest.

Two days later, I found our first dead ewe—a big, beautiful Rambouillet. Only her udder had been eaten. We could see the blood trail through the willows where the ewe had been attacked, tried to flee, and was eventually taken down. A single bite to her throat was her blessed ending.

Wildlife Services was still unsure what species was doing the killing, but had ruled out coyotes. This had to be the work of a bear or wolf. A federal trapper set wolf traps for two nights, in an attempt to catch the predator. I hate traps, but because of the continued kills, Jim and I agreed to the effort, even though it meant containing both the herd and the dogs. Jim and I spent an afternoon setting up a portable pen, and began locking the sheep herd in the pen at night, with the dogs inside with them. It was a scary situation, because if a predator were to get into the pen with the herd, the sheep would not be able to escape. Jim once described to me the carnage left from a black bear that had gotten into his family's sheep barn while the sheep were locked inside. None of these decisions are easy, and they all have risks.

The two nights of trapping proved futile. The predator had either moved on, wasn't showing itself for some reason, or wouldn't come to a baited trap. The sheep had been safe for two days, but we were nervous about the days ahead. The presence of the guardian dogs wasn't enough to protect our herd from a large predator out here in the sagebrush, hundreds of miles from Yellowstone, even when our presence was added to the mix.

As I drove around on another midmorning sheep check, I honked the truck horn to alert the dogs, but the guardians did not appear. They usually come bounding out to greet me. Instead, I could see about twenty ravens circling in the air along the hillside. A big group of ravens is a cause for concern, because it usually means a carcass is present.

I saw the sheep along the bank of the river where they were watering, and hurriedly drove in that direction. As I parked the truck at the edge of a willow stand, Luv's Girl and Rant came racing out at me, huffing and agitated. Obviously something was wrong. They didn't want their food, and when I started to walk toward the willows to investigate, Rant tried to hold me back. At first he placed his body across my path, and when I stepped aside to get around him, he shifted his weight, knocking his hind end against my legs in an attempt to knock me off balance. Intent on finding the source of the ravens' attraction, I shoved him away, but he bounced right back, throwing the weight of his entire body against my thighs, this time knocking me to the ground and whining. My adrenaline was surging at that point, and I regained my footing, shoving my way past the insistent guardian and plunging through the line of willows into the opening near the river. Awaiting me there was blood spatter, part of a sheep rumen, and handful-sized tufts of bloody wool. I instigated a search of the area, with Rant barking aggressively beside me the entire time.

About one hundred yards away from the first scene I found a similar kill site—a rumen, tufts of wool, and a lot of fresh blood. No head, no spine, no ribcage. Two big lambs had been killed. When I breathed in, I could smell the fresh blood in the air, vastly different from the smell of a decaying carcass. My assumption is that the lambs had gone to water early, and were killed there. When the main herd went to water, accompanied by the guardian dogs and burros, the killing was already history—very recent history, from the looks of things.

As I stood in the opening near the river, studying the evidence on the ground, irritated by Rant's frantic woofing, it finally dawned on me that I was alone, unarmed, standing in a place where a large predator had just taken down two of my sheep. I hurried to the safety of the truck, mentally kicking myself for not heeding Rant's warnings, and for being without a gun under these circumstances. Had the guardian stalled my entrance into the willows just long enough to save me from a confrontation with or mauling by the sheep-killing predator? I vowed never again to be so dismissive of my guardians, and I remain thankful for what I believe Rant did for me.

After a few uneventful days, the predator returned. One morning, Jim found another dead ewe. Upon close inspection of the riverbank he also found bear scat, which he showed to our Wildlife Services specialist. Determining that our problems were indeed bear-related, our trapper suggested setting leg snares, using the ewe's carcass as bait.

For our part, Jim and I decided to move the herd out of the pasture —we would push up our shipping schedule to avoid the threat of future losses.

We ended up with three dead ewes and thirteen dead or missing lambs because of our sheep-killing bear, a big increase over our typical seasonal losses. I shudder to think of what the carnage would have been if not for the presence of our livestock protection dogs. The bear was never caught. Our animal-damage-control specialist speculated that it was probably an older male black bear—a bear that had the wisdom of his age.

We weren't the only ones with bear problems out on the range. Vega and Turk, Rant's siblings, managed to team up to attack a black bear that entered their sheep herd as it bedded on the mountain one early morning. Thankfully neither dog was badly injured in the fight. The bear, however, was not so lucky. It would not threaten sheep again. Good, brave guardians.

The loss of livestock to a major predator is an added expense to an ag operation, though thankfully our state wildlife agency provides some compensation for damages due to trophy-game-species predation, including black bears.

Our predator losses are small when compared to those experienced by my friend Mary Thoman. Her family has grazed their sheep on four allotments in the Upper Green River region of western Wyoming for decades, but there has been a pattern of increased conflicts in recent years as wolf and grizzly bear populations continue to increase. The ranch places three herds of about one thousand head of sheep on the allotments for grazing from July through September each year, leaving one allotment to rest. Mary's family uses about six livestock protection dogs with each herd of sheep, but the large predators have wounded and killed several of her dogs on several occasions.

One of the allotments was frequented by twelve grizzly bears and four black bears in 2010. In addition, wildlife managers killed two black bears in response to depredation problems. Two grizzly bear sows and their cubs harassed a second sheep herd. State wildlife officials removed two wolves and one grizzly bear from this herd. A third sheep herd had two or three grizzly bears, six wolves, and a mountain lion around it all summer. The sheep were safe at night while they were locked in the safety of a portable electric pen, but these big predators were successful in preying on the herds in daylight hours.

Mary told me that the major killing occurred during the daytime, when small groups of sheep were run up into the timber or rocks. In 2010, predators killed 259 ewes and 186 lambs from Mary's herds, with a total value of about $65,000. The Thomans received nearly $54,000 in damage compensation from the Wyoming Game and Fish Department, with the ranch forced to absorb the remaining $11,000 loss on its own.

Livestock losses due to large carnivores on the allotments have increased steadily in recent years, with damage ranging from about $17,000 in 2005, to $40,000 in 2008, and 2010's $65,000. Mary said that while the ranch had made adjustments to try to control losses, the arrival of female grizzlies with cubs resulted in a doubling of livestock losses.

One of the Thoman's sheepherders was mauled by a grizzly bear during the 2009 grazing season when he stepped away from his tent to check on a barking livestock-protection dog one night. He survived, but was badly injured.

The Thomans use livestock protection dogs that have proven to be very effective against male grizzlies, but have limited effectiveness with bear family groups, and with wolves. Wolves killed four of the Thoman guardian dogs in 2004.

Dangerous as the situation can get, I'll take my black bear problems over Mary's grizzlies any day. I just don't know how long her family can sustain such losses and stay in business. One year like that would force my marginal operation off the range.

⟡   ⟡   ⟡   ⟡

Cass and I straddled our dirt bikes to ride the pasture looking for any sheep that had strayed from the flock during the day, while Jim slowly pushed one small bunch of sheep toward Waterhole Draw. We joined up there, allowing the sheep to enjoy a short rest and long sating drink of water before we began the push to the north into a smaller neighboring pasture where the sheep would be easier to gather the next morning. It was an all-day gather and move, and we were all tired when we left the herd for the night.

Early the next morning, we gathered the herd once again, and pushed them into the newly erected shipping pen. Each sheep was handled and moved down the chute, with lambs pushed out a cutting gate into a separate pen.

Once we'd sorted the lambs from the ewes, we loaded the lambs into livestock trailers for transport. They would be weighed, and then placed in a holding pasture in preparation for sale to an Idaho lamb buyer. Loading and transporting lambs is an arduous operation. They weigh between eighty and ninety pounds by now, and they are not happy about being separated from their mothers. They show little affection for humans at this point. They are spooked by the trailer, and by the shadows in the pen, so loading them requires both patience and muscle, while we work outside under a bright sun with a brisk wind kicking sand and grit into our eyes. Then it's a long slow drive pulling the trailer so the babes have a gentle ride. We weighed the last load of lambs as the sun was setting and added them to the holding pasture using the headlights of the pickup truck to light the way. By the time our truck rolled back into the driveway at home it was 11 P.M. and we were weary, with two dogs snoring on the seat in cramped quarters between Jim and me.

We were up early the next day to do it again. While we had sorted lambs from the ewes to go to market, we had also sorted off the very best ewe lambs to be retained for the herd. Ewes too old or weary were sorted to go to sale as well. We hauled the ewes to their new pas-

Tiny lambs just a few months prior, the lambs are now
large and fat and ready to be shipped.

ture, just under an hour's driving distance away. The ewes were much
easier to handle and load than the lambs, since they have done it before and would rather comply than resist. It took the entire day to get
all the animals—sheep, burros, and dogs—safety transported to their
new pasture, on private property in the boulder-strewn foothills of the
Wind River Mountains. The sheep would stay on open hillsides, avoid-

ing the timber and cover provided by the mountainside, as well as the river bottom. A few more months of grazing in the foothills and the ewe herd will return to the home ranch for winter feeding.

Shortly after the ewes return home, their rams will join them for breeding. There are fantastic battles for breeding rights between these great beasts. Huge and muscular, they weigh between three hundred and four hundred pounds, and have thick horns that curl out away from their heads. The rams know exactly where their horn tips are and how to use them if they feel threatened. They respond to the onset of cold weather, sensing that breeding season is coming. One November day a few years ago, I heard a tremendous crash—it sounded like a truck hitting a wooden building—and stepped out the back door to see one heck of a ram fight. Two of the rams were really going at it, with a third joining in. All were bloody and battered. Rena tried to stop them, and I rushed at them, throwing rocks, to no avail. I ended up using the truck to intervene, trying to nudge them apart, but they were adamant about wanting to fight, knocking each other to their knees. I finally got them to run, and pushed them out into the sagebrush. They are fierce beasts, and sometimes these fights turn deadly. I once saw a young ram battering an older ram until the old ram's back was broken.

The sheep herd will spend the winter days following a feed line of alfalfa hay laid fresh daily at the ranch, and five months later, it will be time for lambing to begin again.

Although most sheep return from mountain pastures in the fall with no fanfare, small symbolic festivals are held in a few communities in the western United States, including Idaho's Trailing of the Sheep festival, which takes place in October. The goal of the festival, which features food, dance, and regional artisans, is to gather, present, and preserve the history and culture of the sheep industry in that state. The Trailing of the Sheep parade is a 150-year-old tradition.

Austria celebrates the end of the grazing season with festivals as well. In mid-September, herds return from their summer mountain pastures to the lowlands, and the citizens of Gschnitz and Pfons celebrate with food, drink, music, and other entertainment. These events are held to mark the importance of the return of as few as one hundred cows and calves and three hundred sheep. I love the idea that the return of the sheep is celebrated, wherever in the world it occurs. They have journeyed, had adventures, and now have come home.

As we pulled my empty camp out of the pasture at the end of the season, the sun was starting to set, and the overwhelming sense of relief at a job well done was tinged with sadness. My heart resides on the range, and with those animals that shared my life there. Jim and I will hold our own celebration tonight, thankful for nature's bounty, and for its kindness to my herd.

I look forward to the day in the very near future when the herd will join me at home. Like my days on the range, the best days are those in which I wake up to see the herd with each sunrise and go to sleep knowing they are nearby.

But tonight I'll dream about it. The sun will rise and Assistant Sheep will respond to my morning call in her unique voice, running forward to lead the herd to a new year.